RICH MAN POOR MAN

Donald W. Shriver, Jr.

CARTOONS BY JIM CRANE

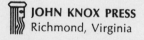 JOHN KNOX PRESS
Richmond, Virginia

Library of Congress Cataloging in Publication Data

Shriver, Donald W
   Rich man poor man.
   (Christian ethics for modern man)   (Chime paperbacks)
   Bibliography: p.
   1. Christianity and economics. 2. Christian ethics.
I. Title.
BR115.E3S47   261.8'5   71-37003
ISBN 0-8042-9092-X

General Editor's Foreword

Christian Ethics for Modern Man is a series of brief and easy-to-read books on moral issues in contemporary social problems. The books do not provide or pretend to provide the Christian with answers to the complex problems confronting modern man. They do offer guidance to Christians searching for their own answers. The purpose of the series is to help persons make moral judgments more responsibly.

Decisions! Decisions! by George A. Chauncey analyzes the elements that go into any moral judgment and suggests ways one's faith in God can, ought to, and sometimes does influence his moral decisions.

Rich Man Poor Man by Donald W. Shriver, Jr., discusses some of the moral issues American Christians face as they participate in and benefit from the American economy. The book incorporates and comments on recorded conversations among Christian theologians, businessmen, labor leaders, and consumers on those moral issues.

Foreign Policy Is Your Business by Theodore R. Weber examines some of the moral issues faced by a government and its citizens in the development and conduct of foreign policy. Examples: Under what conditions ought a nation go to war? How should the U.S.A. relate to Communist governments? Is it ever right for a government to deceive its own citizens?

These books have been written not only for individual study but also for group discussion. *Leader's Guide to Christian Ethics for Modern Man* by Richard F. Perkins offers valuable suggestions for the use of these books by groups.

George A. Chauncey
GENERAL EDITOR

CONTENTS

1. Moral Judgments on Economic Issues:
   A Stroll Through History   7
2. Faith, Fact, and Norm:
   A Recipe for Judgment-Making   16
3. Money:
   My Master or God's Servant?   37
4. Competition:
   Does It Build or Destroy?   54
5. The Rich and the Poor:
   What Is the Justice of God in an Unjust World?   81
6. Postscript:
   The Pilgrimage of Christian Ethical Reflection   105

1 | MORAL JUDGMENTS ON ECONOMIC ISSUES: A Stroll Through History

In a playful moment, getting ready to write these pages, I imagined myself taking a time machine back into history and stopping off to interview an assortment of people on the question: "On the whole, sir, what moral judgments do you make on issues in your local economy?"

First stop was the house of a cloth manufacturer in sixteenth century Swiss Geneva.

"The two best things that have happened in this city in a hundred years have both happened within my memory. First, those theologians finally decided that renting *money* is not much different from renting houses. We have a flourishing banking business here now, and we don't have to go running to the Jews or the Florentines anymore to get capital. Of course, merchants in Geneva managed to charge interest on their money in one way or another for quite a while before the late John Calvin came. But it has greatly helped commerce and industry to know that the church no longer tells the people that 'usury' is of the devil. The preachers still rail at us for charging too high a rate, but at least they no longer balk at the idea.

"That's one reason I moved here from France in the 1550's, by the way: it's a good place for new businesses. An intelligent, ambitious type of person tends to make his way to Geneva, so the supply of good workers has much improved. That's the second good thing from a commercial point of view. This used to be a pretty de-

praved place. Prostitution was the big money-maker, not
manufacturing. Quite a moral improvement, don't you
think?"

Second stop: a wooden hut with a straw roof, near a
Norman castle in southern England: Time: early in the
twelfth century. The interviewee is a serf of the lord of
the castle, and the interview is short.

"What kind of a question is that? Nobody asks a serf
to make judgments on anything. You must be from somewhere else. All I know is that when the Normans took
over, they made us work one more month for them, raised
their share of the crops by half, and closed the forest
where we used to collect our firewood. A lot of good it
will do to make judgments on all that. I just hope that my
five children don't freeze this winter."

Third stop: with a member of a religious sect called
"Followers of the Way," "Nazarenes," or "Christians," in
the city of Antioch on the eastern end of the Mediter-
ranean Sea. It is A.D. 55.

"I suppose you mean what changes we Christians try
to make in our use of material things. We don't try to tell
anybody else how they should act about material things.
This is a corrupt society, you know. The Romans and
their friends have the money, the fine houses, and the
rich food. But we Christians know that all this is idolatry.
God will bring it all under *his* judgment soon, so we don't
have to make judgments on it. We have enough to do to
make some changes in the way we Christians use our few
material goods.

"Only there's a growing dispute among us over this
very thing. Some say that twenty years ago the Jerusalem
Christians really set the example: all material goods were

given to the community, and everybody used the common treasury as he had need. But did you know that it fell apart even in Jerusalem? Here we just have a Poor Fund to which most members give what they can. Out of that fund we also support the apostles' journeys to other parts of the Empire. But some still argue for the common treasury. But it really doesn't matter; the Lord will be returning soon, we won't need either a treasury or a Poor Fund. Still, if you are a Christian, I'd be interested in knowing your view of this matter."

My visits are too brief for conversation. Back another 800 years in time, I trudge alongside a farmer on the road to the small city of Bethel, on the border between the states of Israel and Judah. Four donkeys follow him, carrying sixteen baskets of wheat.

"Well, stranger, it's a little hard to explain; but the thing we all talk about back home is whether there's any way to stop taking our wheat to Bethel. Things have changed so much since I was a boy. Once we traded our surplus grain for shoes and cloth in the village. Hardly anybody ever saw a piece of money. Then the merchants started offering what seemed like high prices in the market at Bethel, and we began bringing grain up here. But lately some of us have been wishing for the old days, when there wasn't any money. One of my neighbors actually *sold his land for money* last year to one of the merchants. Imagine, my neighbor has sold a piece of the land that the Lord promised us from Egypt!

"And what's just as terrible, the wheat in these baskets will be sold to poor people in Bethel for five times what the merchants will pay me for it. They say that it's none of my business what they charge: 'We buy and sell at market prices.' So poor farmers get gobbled up, and poor widows go hungry! It makes me ashamed to have anything to do with Bethel. What do you think, stranger? Should I stay at home, weave my own cloth, and make my own shoes?"

But I'm off to my last stop. I'm in a small village of people with reddened skins, living in tents of animal hides. We are in a green, wooded valley beside a mountain stream. The people call themselves "Atali Tsalagi," and the time machine translates that, "Upper Cherokees." Though the machine has no difficulty identifying words in any language that correspond to words in my own, the difficulty of communication here is greater than at any other stop; many words just don't match up. One elderly red man finally says:

"Is the stranger asking if we are at peace with the Bear, the Fish, the Eagle, and the Buffalo? Yes, we are at peace with them. How else could we live? The forest is our home, the animals are our brothers, and what happens to them happens to us. We kill them when we need their life, and sometimes they kill us. But the Great Spirits have made us friends. Our only enemies live across the hills. They walk on two feet like ourselves. Once, long ago, they came over the mountain to take away our valley, but the Bear, the Fish, the Eagle, and the Buffalo fought with us and we won. Once every twelve moons we make ourselves strong with that victory; it is the best of all times, a great festival. Since you are a stranger, you would not be welcome then. Did you come from across the hills too?"

*   *   *

At first glance, this flight of fancy may seem utterly remote from the affairs of the twentieth century; indeed, one point of beginning this way is to suggest that "moral judgments on economic issues" have not been the same in every age and in every society. Human times and societies have exhibited some fantastic differences in their understanding of what an "economic issue" is, and of how it is related to everything else in a human life.

Since the area under discussion in this book is "the American economy," it might give us a preliminary focus on that area to note some points of contact between American economic realities and those of the fictional interviews just conducted.

1. *We think of "economic" as a special segment of our life.* Communication with the pre-Columbus Cherokee Indian on economic issues is bound to be hard, because the Cherokee, like all his Stone Age brethren in Africa, Europe, and the rest of this planet, did not separate life into pieces. This is a habit rather lately acquired in the history of civilization. During most of human history, men did not think about their relation to their physical world ("nature") apart from their relation to their spiritual world ("religion") or to their social organization ("economics, politics, etc."). As our eighth century Judean farmer suggests, one of the ways by which economic life got split off in men's minds from the rest of life was through the invention of *money*. Some other ways were the invention of means of travel and the exchange of surplus physical goods.

It is a long, complicated story, but it is worth remembering that there was a time when the majority of men would not know what we moderns mean by our "economic issues." Like the Genevan merchant, we can talk casually about interest rates, wage rates, and unemployment rates without feeling that, at the same time, we are talking about

political policies, religious beliefs, or moral principles. For
the Cherokee, that was impossible. For the Judean farmer,
it was hard. For the Genevan merchant, it was becoming
easy; and it was this, among other things, that made us
feel instinctively that he was close to being a "modern
man."

2. *We are used to living in a relatively large economic system.* The noted anthropologist Margaret Mead
remarked once that she had spent most of her life studying
South Pacific tribesmen who did not know how to
organize a society larger than five hundred people. Groups
not even that large have been the rule in most of human
history. Only in the past few thousand years have great
empires—China, Egypt, Assyria, and the like—risen up to
bind millions together politically and economically. Only
within the past five hundred years has there been such a
thing as global trade relations. And world distribution
of products like Coca Cola and IBM computers is a
phenomenon that has occurred mostly within the lifetimes
of people reading this book.

Among other things, this vast increase in the size of

our economic systems has meant a sharp decline in the "face to face" nature of men's economic relationships. Gone from the lives of most Americans is the small, production-and-exchange community of the forest tribe, the feudal manor, or the crossroads market. The very idea that we should have personal relationships with the people who produce our food, repair our cars, and manufacture our clothes is often regarded as quaint and old-fashioned.

One neighbor complains that she has had coffee ground at a local A & P store for some six years by the same lady, but the lady has yet to indicate any personal recognition of this regular customer. But more striking yet is the fact that there is hardly any way by which the producers of those coffee beans—Brazilian farmers—can become "real persons" to customers at that coffee counter. The coffee-marketing system is too large for that. It is also too large for most people affected by that market even to *imagine* each other. How many Americans know what it is like to be a Brazilian farmer?

Of course, the presence of actual persons in economic transactions is no less real in today's global economic systems than in yesterday's village markets. But the impersonal appearance of factories, distribution systems, and price systems inclines many of us to divorce "systems" from people.

3. *Few of us share agreements on what "the" issues of our economic system are.* What any human being sees is a result partly of where he stands or sits. This is as true of one's feel for "moral issues" in a society as it is true of your seat in a theater or stadium.

For example, a voyage back into time to look at past economic systems would be of little contemporary interest but for one fact: almost every person in my fictional interviews has a viewpoint that resembles profoundly the viewpoint of some person in our own American society.

The Genevan merchant's outlook on interest rates and the labor market can be found in every local Chamber of Commerce in America. The medieval manor serf, bound to a particular plot of land and perpetually in debt to the landowner, is not far from the sharecroppers who still can be found in counties in the American South.

The Judean farmer's mixed feelings about getting tangled up in a money market and his fear of losing his land to a businessman has a counterpart in the family farm owner who must sell out to "agri-business" in order to survive in the face of industrialized farming methods. As for the Antioch Christians, in America we still have some groups of Christians (such as the Amish in Pennsylvania) who have tried to set up self-sufficient economic communities in order to avoid contamination with what they regard as the worldly, greedy, and unchristian society around them.

As for the Cherokees, we have in many parts of the United States groups who have abandoned the national economic system for communes, tribal living, and other forms of revolt against a style of life which they regard as corrupt. Many of these latter groups are seeking to re-establish the harmony between themselves and nature which they see in Stone Age man.

The *contrast* between all these viewpoints on economic affairs and certain other viewpoints available in modern America is of course easy to recognize. Indeed, if we visited some neighbors in our own hometowns we would meet some people who, economically speaking, are historical newcomers: the elderly man who fears the effect of inflation on his social security check; the space scientist who loses his job from the cutback after Apollo 14; and perhaps thousands of other people who work in the 30,000 job classifications which have been identified, most of which did not exist a hundred years ago. This suggests that the discussion of modern economic affairs cannot strictly parallel discussions in previous centuries of human history.

All of this, however, does not define the idea of "viewpoint" very precisely. What makes up a modern American's viewpoint on economic affairs? How does a viewpoint get constructed, and, where there is a choice between viewpoints, what should determine or influence the choice? Are there right and wrong viewpoints from which to look out over the landscape of economic affairs in the United States? Or is the whole discussion of better and worse viewpoints a waste of time?

Such questions are so important that they deserve a chapter of their own before we get down to some exploration of "moral judgments on issues in the American economy." We need to ask ourselves what moral judgments are and what our viewpoints have to do with making them.

2 | FAITH, FACT, AND NORM: A Recipe for Judgment-Making

In the mid-1960's, the Presbyterian Church in the United States sent this writer to the World Conference on Church and Society, sponsored by the World Council of Churches. At this conference many questions about economic affairs around the world were discussed. In particular, the economic needs of the world's poor, in relation to the world's rich, received abundant attention.

On my return I gathered together a group of businessmen, and for an evening we discussed the question of the relation of the rich and poor people in the modern world. Midway in the discussion, I commented: "One of the general beliefs that many people in this conference affirmed was the biblical idea that, whenever there is a choice between meeting the needs of the rich and the needs of the poor, the priority should always be with the poor." The seven American businessmen expressed such disagreement with the statement that out of curiosity I called for a vote. Who accepts and who rejects this general principle? The vote was five to two to reject it.

On the side of rejecting the principal lay some forthright arguments:

We live in a competitive world.

The poor of other countries are beyond our capacity to help.

A man must put the welfare of his own family first.

On the side of accepting it lay some similarly forthright arguments:

The Old Testament prophets thought so.

We are required to love our neighbors in the whole human race.

It's simple justice to put the poor man's needs first.

What is involved here? Something similar to what is involved when a group of people decide whether they will play basketball or football: the *nature* of the game, the *rules* by which it will be played, and all the other *assumptions* that must be settled before there can be any game. (Whereas "nature" and "rules" are often explicitly spelled out somewhere, our "assumptions" may well be things which we "just know" are true and which we assume "everybody" believes. But because we have never explicitly stated them, even to ourselves, we *might* have a hard time defending or substantiating them if forced to do so. In the interviews in chapter 1, the assumptions or viewpoints of those interviewed are frequently quite apparent, and almost as frequently they would *not* be the assumptions that you and I work from.)

It is about the nature, rules, and assumptions of the "economic game" in the United States of America that this book will be repeatedly concerned. That makes it from the start a rather discomforting little volume. This study is written to be read by adults, and the very process of uncovering basic assumptions is rather uncomfortable. An actual interview with a Wintu Indian in California some years ago, for example, contained these vivid words describing the difference between the western white man's assumptions about his rightful relation to nature and those of the Indian:

. . . the white people plow up the ground, pull up the trees, kill everything. The tree says, "Don't. I am

sore. Don't hurt me." But they chop it down and
cut it up. The spirit of the land hates them. . . .
How can the spirit of the earth like the white man?
. . . Everywhere the white man has touched it, it is
sore.[1]

Something more than differences in economic tech-
niques is being identified here. Conflicts over what are the
good, proper, and right relations between men and their
environment are at stake. Disconcertingly basic questions
are at stake. What *is* a tree? Is it the home of a spirit?
a home for squirrels? construction material for human
housing? an object to be enjoyed as beautiful? an obstacle
to roadbuilding? a source of oxygen for the atmosphere?

Is a tree—or a valley, or a stream—subject to human
"ownership"? What right has any human being to consider a piece of the earth as his own? What is the standard
for determining the owner of a particular material object?

This country was
nothing before
I came.

Useless trees,
empty land, rivers
and mountains.

I cut the trees,
filled the land,
bulldozed the
mountains.

Is it the one who can pay the highest price in money, or who has the most effective military force, or who can convince the other that his ancestors owned it? Given a certain cluster of material things, what is their relative importance? Is a fruit tree to be preferred to a nugget of gold?

When there is a question of who should have the privilege of eating the fruit of the tree, how is the choice to be made? If some human being is to die from starvation, how shall he be chosen? Are such matters just left to "fate," so that one man "happens" to starve while another "happens" to live? And as for living or starving, does that make any difference? Is it as well for a man to die as to live? Under what circumstances is it preferable to die, preferable to live?

The list of such questions quickly gets very long and very *oppressive* as well. What an intolerable task it is to have to think through *all* the assumptions that lie slumber-

I put in the tracts, the hot dog stands, and put the rivers to good use removing sewage.

This country owes me a lot. I made the jobs.

It was a damn good country too, before the bleeding hearts and socialists started ruining things.

ing underneath one's day-to-day existence! Indeed, the
task of digging up those assumptions is one that only a
minority of human beings in history has ever undertaken.
(Most men have believed what someone else told them,
then built their lives on these allegedly solid beliefs. Yet
in reality men's assumptions about their relationship to
their material environment are subject to vast changes,
as our imaginary trip back into time reminds us.)

Today, however, the changes going on are causing
people in unprecedented numbers to dig up old assumptions and to look at them. They are doing so because they
increasingly see that the general beliefs one brings to the
beginning of every waking day have specific consequences
in moment after moment of that day. This is as true of a
man's life-sustaining relations with his material environment as of any other relations. (The psychologist Kurt
Lewin once said: "Nothing is so practical as a good
theory." Translate that into the tree illustration above,
and you get: "Whether and how trees are an 'economic
issue' depends on whether you define a tree as a home of
a spirit, a source of oxygen, or one of your investments.")

This study cannot be the occasion for any reader to
dig up all of his elusive assumptions about economic
affairs. The aim is really more modest: to set the reader on
the way toward such digging, and to help him to dig from
one particular angle, the angle of moral judgment-making.

But this very statement of purpose itself contains
quite a burden of assumptions, so let me spell them out
a bit further.

Toward Making Moral Judgments

Socrates once said, "The unexamined life is not
worth living." He said this in a time when his country
was undergoing certain changes that made it hard for

him, at least, to avoid asking "basic questions." Ordinary, routine times tend to cover up such questions from the inquiry of the great majority of people in a society. Life in the Appalachian forest had become routine for the Cherokee, but in meeting the white man the Indian had to cope with the intrusion of new attitudes toward trees and toward the ownership of property. Life for the Judean farmer was routine, perhaps, until he had to reckon with the intrusion of a growing money economy.

In many ways we in the latter part of the twentieth century have more reason to be conscious of changes in human routine than many other generations. We are the ones who live in a world most of which some nations could destroy in a flash, where news travels at the speed of light, where knowledge doubles every ten years. These non-routine actualities and possibilities readily throw us back into "why" questions that are both hard and vital to answer.

This is especially so the more *decisions about action* any man is called upon to make in the midst of a non-routine world. Of the people from history whom we interviewed, the medieval serf and the Cherokee did not see themselves as involved in much decision-making in this area of their lives. They seemed to assume most of the decisions had already been made.

But not so the others, and not so you and me. It is said that the modern driver of an automobile in city traffic makes forty decisions a minute—all such decisions based upon a complex combination of the driver's attention to traffic laws, the physical dynamics of steering, his expectations of other drivers, and his perceptions of changing traffic patterns in relation to his own and others' safety.

The automobile, in fact, is a good illustration of how

changes in modern society push many of us to consider
some changes in our basic assumptions. Many people
reading these words long thought of the auto as a sign
of the privilege of living in a rich country. Within the last
few years, however, large numbers of Americans have
become disenchanted with cars. What is the value of a car
alongside (*a*) the worth of the 55,000 people who were
killed in 1970 by the machine, (*b*) the value of the clean
air which is now being polluted chiefly by internal com-
bustion engines, and (*c*) the value of cheaper, safer,
quicker forms of travel that modern technology might
provide us?

But even more basic value assumptions are now being
raised on many sides concerning the automobile and its
role in the American economy. By what right do Americans burn fourteen million gallons of gasoline a day, half
the world's available supplies of petroleum, thus reducing
those supplies at a rate which may leave them utterly ex-
hausted on a global scale before the year 2025? Is it a
humanly enriching thing that the average American moves
around some five thousand miles annually? What is the
measure of a rich rather than a poor human life, anyway?

If your personal answer to this last question, by the
way, is simply: "How much money one has in the bank,"
you are probably reading the wrong book; I recommend
that you lay it gently aside! If, on the other hand, you are
intrigued by the question of the right of Americans to half
the world's petroleum; if you are frankly puzzled by the
question of what makes any man "truly rich" or "truly
poor"; if you wonder whether you yourself know what
real worthiness is in human relationships; and if you
would like to identify for yourself some root reasons for
judging any man richly or poorly human, then read on!

The writer of this volume and its other contributors share a common curiosity about these things. Their thought-trains run back from the branches of their daily involvement in American economic life to the roots and subsoil of their reasons for such involvement. In those roots and in that subsoil are those foundations of economic relationships to which some would give the name *ethics*. But others would dig a little deeper and call the deepest foundation *faith*.

Fact, Faith, and Principle

The Wintu Indian who condemns the white man's treatment of the natural world is making a moral judgment upon him. More: he is making a religiously grounded moral judgment. A similar judgment was being made by our Judean farmer upon his neighbor who sold his land to the Bethel merchant. That merchant, and his colleagues two thousand years later in Geneva, would probably have scoffed at this judgment and said: "Why, if a man wants to sell his own property, that's *his* business, isn't it?"

One may think so, if one also thinks that there is such a reality as "private property." Most Indians did not think that there was such a reality. When they "sold" Manhattan Island to the Dutch, they probably thought that they were selling hunting and fishing rights for a few years. And the Hebrews did not think that there was such a reality, either; the promised land belonged to the nation whose Lord their God had brought them up out of Egypt. Such are the "myths" (if you don't believe in them) or the "deepest human convictions" (if you do) by which we human beings *interpret* and *understand* the everyday reality of our lives.

One can look at the matter of "deep" convictions in

other ways than through the analogy to tree roots. Take
any activity in which you engage and see how long you
can keep asking yourself the question, "Why?" about this
activity. If a child in your household has ever made a
game out of this process, you know that it can be an
elfish game for a child, a frustrating game for the adult.

"Daddy, why do you go to work every day?"

"To earn the money for our family, son."

"Why do you do that?"

"Because we all have to eat."

"Why?"

"Because if we didn't eat we'd die."

"Why?"

"Because that's the way our bodies work."

"Why?"

"Why? Well, I don't know. That's the way God made
things to be. Everybody, everything needs food
to live."

"Why?"

"Because everything that lives wants to keep on
living."

"Why?"

"I told you why: God made it that way, too. Now
run along and play."

"Why?"

*"Because I told you, and if you don't I'll swat you
with this newspaper."*

Why *does* a man go to work every day? Some possible reasons are suggested in this hypothetical child-
parent interchange. There are other reasons that might be
offered, of course, and if one tries to deal with the sum
total of reasons, he will probably recognize significant
differences in *kinds* of reasons. For example:

To earn money—an *economic* reason.

We all have to eat—a *biological* reason.

We want to keep on living—a *psychological* reason.

Because in this country a man doesn't feel that he is a real man if he doesn't work—another psychological reason, relating to a particular human *culture*.

Because the government will take me to court for nonsupport of my family if I don't at least try to get a job—a *legal-political* reason.

Because God has given me the strength and intelligence to work, and it would be poor stewardship for me not to use his gifts to me—a *religious* reason.

I feel obligated to be a good worker—a *moral* reason, that could easily be rooted in the religious reason above.

Because I love you—either a *religious* or a *moral* reason, depending on whether these words are part of (*a*) a prayer or (*b*) a conversation with another human being.

(Is it possible, by the way, that many a child plays the "why game" with his parents because he is fishing for some fundamental reason like the last one? If a child ever does play that game with you, it would be interesting to note if this last reason cuts the game short in his mind. He could go on: "But why do you love me, Daddy?" Most parents cannot answer that question without saying, in effect, what their real religion is. A simple, basically Christian answer would be: "Because God loves me, son, and other people, too.")

The importance of the reasons you affirm for doing *anything* is obviously no merely theoretical matter. If, for example, a man's job is killing him through an ulcer, his doctor may advise him to change jobs or even to retire. In this case for a biological reason he may change his relation to the economic system. On the other hand, his concern that his child get a college education may, because of his ambition and love, make him defy the biological law of self-preservation and risk death itself by staying on the job. One sort of reason has taken back seat to another sort. *The reasons you rather consistently put in the front seat of your decision-making is the stuff of your religion and ethics.*

In this sense, any one of the reasons above could operate as "religion and ethics" for you: "to make money" can be the sum and substance of your religion, the commanding principle of your ethic. To help discover your own religious and ethical foundations, ask the following about any reason you give for a decision: Can I think of any *better* reason for deciding this way?

Ethical Analysis

Some would call it an intellectual game, but "ethical analysis"—what we have in fact begun to do above—is an exceedingly serious, unavoidable game. Serious, in that it literally concerns life-and-death matters; unavoidable, because every human being has decisions to make about such matters. Some form of ethical analysis goes on in everybody's mind when the following happens:

1. A choice has to be made among alternatives for action. (When there is really "only one thing to do," "no choice in the matter," then there is no possibility for ethical analysis.)

2. The choice requires some judgment about the relationship between the facts in the case and convictions about what is good, right, or proper human behavior. (There usually are many things that could be done and many possible evaluations of alternatives, depending on what that decision-maker thinks is good, right, or proper human behavior.)

Working at the relating of "facts" and one's ideas about the "good, right, and proper" is the heart of ethical analysis. Take the decision that a man or woman faces in response to the offer of a new job. What is the salary? the working conditions? the ability required? (Matters of fact) What salary do I need to realize my aims in life? (Both "need" and "aims" involve some notions of what is good, right, or proper.) What sort of work do I enjoy the most? (Factual) What sort of work does my family want me to do? (Factual) Is it good, or right, or proper for me to do the work that I happen to enjoy the most or the work that happens to pay the most? (A question of personal ethics) Should I pay most attention to what my family wants, what I want, what my company wants, what our whole society wants? (A question of social ethics) What does God want me to do?

If one believes in God, the possibility that we can get an answer to that last question appears to be a great blessing. If God is, and if he communicates with men, then a word from him will cut short all this business of ethical analysis! But there are not many people who believe that all the other questions can be avoided by simply giving attention to the last one.

In Victor Hugo's novel *Les Miserables,* for example, the hero Jean Valjean is a good Christian, but on one occasion he decides to steal bread to feed his starving

children. Did God want him to steal? As a citizen he had
all his life obeyed the law against stealing; now love for
his children took precedence. He made a decision to dis-
obey one law in order to obey what some would call the
"higher law" of compassion. And one of the ethical issues
of the novel is whether there is any higher law than strict
justice, whether forgiveness and mercy on occasion must
take precedence over "even-handed justice."

Obviously such an issue can only be resolved in
terms of what a man ultimately believes: his religion. But
few wise Christians, few wise men of any religious tradition, think that one can resort to *religious* reasons for
doing something while totally ignoring *factual* and *ethical*
reasons. No reader of the Hugo novel is likely to make a
judgment of Valjean's action without juggling in his mind
such questions as (1) the importance of obeying the law,
(2) the relative importance of laws protecting private property over against laws protecting children from starvation,
(3) whether society should have a policy of feeding hungry
children, and (4) what a father is justified in doing in a
society that has no such policy. *All* of these questions cry
out for some answers in the form of *ethical guidelines,*
or what have traditionally been called *ethical principles.*
Examples of ethical principles relevant to making a judgment on Valjean's action would be:

Laws must be obeyed even if justice is denied.

Justice must be done even if laws must be disobeyed
to achieve justice.

One wrong is no excuse for doing another wrong.

The need of children for bread sometimes must take
precedence over the need of bakeries to keep
their profits up.

Government has an obligation to protect shopkeepers from thievery *and* children from starvation.

The sum of all this complex business is this: when men make important choices, they have negotiations (1) with facts, (2) with principles, and, underneath it all, (3) with a faith. Usually we find these assorted elements of moral judgment-making mixed up together. But the job of ethical analysis is to separate them and, we hope, to put them back together in better shape.

To help reader and writer do that in relation to "issues in the American economy," this book is written.

Putting It All Together

At the risk of being repetitious and obvious, I now offer you a set of definitions appropriate to this study of moral judgments on issues in the American economy. Long books have been written on every one of the terms defined here. This is a short book, so I leave all the definitions but the last in their brevity here. Later on in this study there will be further light thrown on these definitions.

ECONOMY: "The conditions and laws affecting the production, distribution, and consumption of wealth, or the material means of satisfying human desires." (Webster)

MORAL PRINCIPLE: A rule or general standard for evaluating human actions. Usually it relates to the impact of a personal or group action upon another person or group. Moral principles usually concern what is good or bad, right or wrong, proper or improper in human behavior. Notions about justice, happiness, or the rights of man are examples of moral principles.

ISSUE: An occasion for decision growing out of an

apparent conflict between two or more possible courses of action, priorities, or principles for guiding action. No event in human society becomes an issue until it forces someone to choose between one priority or another. An *economic* issue forces a choice between alternate uses of resources (goods or services or money). A *moral issue* forces a choice between giving priority to a moral principle (such as justice) or to some other value (such as law). And *moral issues in economic affairs* are often issues that force participants to make judgments about the use of economic resources by reference to one or more moral principles or measures.

MORAL JUDGMENT-MAKING: The process or procedure by which an individual or group of people arrive at a decision on a moral issue. In this study we shall assume that the ingredients of a moral judgment are at least three: (1) a set of facts; (2) one or more principles or norms stating what is good or bad, right or wrong, proper or improper, in human behavior; and (3) a reference by the judgment-maker to some ultimate source of measurement and meaning for human behavior, a reference that may be called *faith*. The major intellectual task in making moral judgments is the hard work of fitting together one's perception of fact, awareness of principle, and commitment of faith.

It is the very last element of the last definition that deserves a little more attention here. The definition asserts that there is an "ultimate" present somehow in moral reasoning. No moral judgment-making escapes some dependence, however indirect, upon a religious faith. Before getting down to "the issues," an additional word about religion and how religious faith will inevitably shape what a man thinks the issues are may be helpful.

A Confession of Faith

We have said that one's reasoning about his decisions must, like digging for China, stop somewhere. At the bottom of every chain of why's, the human mind finds itself saying: "Here I stand, I can do no other." Going to work in the morning as usual, or committing suicide instead, are actions equally and ultimately dependent upon such a last link in the chain.

This is not to say what should be the nature of that last link. As modern Americans, many readers of this study may suspect that they are at home in a post-religious age. Even as a member of a church, you may have honestly reflected to yourself, while listening to a sermon one Sunday, that this oldtime Hebrew and Christian view of things is out of touch with contemporary reality. The economic world you live in—wages, hours, salaries, stocks, interest rates, expanding and contracting markets, cost reductions—is not the economic world of the Bible! And the old beliefs about promised land, corrupt Babylonian or Roman society, and the imminent end of the world don't fit your times.

What beliefs are fit, then, for you and your times? What is your view of the world—what *is* the world, and how does it really relate to you? That may be a very hard question for you to answer. But as we have already begun to suspect, such a question is not irrelevant to anyone's study of moral judgments on issues in the American economy. This study will have failed to penetrate to really basic issues if it does not help you clarify your own answer to this sort of question. Mark it down as an always hovering motive behind the pages to follow: to help every reader decide in his own mind what the last link in his why-line is; what sort of ultimate commitment is at the root of his life.

It is only fair, it seems to me, to end these introductory chapters with an attempt by the author to say, as best he can, what the end of the why-line is for me. To say that is not easy. How can we be sure what the real foundations of any man's behavior are, especially if the behavior is one's own? Readers of the book *The Christian Life,* by Waldo Beach, will remember that in its first chapter, "Christianity in Suburbia," there is a recital of what Beach suggests as the "real creed" of many middle-class American Christians. In part that creed says:

> . . . I believe everyone has a right to economic security and a high standard of living (especially me and my family), gained by individual effort and initiative and luck. I believe in staying busy and acquiring more gadgets to make life convenient and pleasant and to get places faster. . . . I believe that it is better to be young than old, better to be moving than still, better to be comfortable than uncomfortable, better to be rich than poor. . . .[2]

What philosopher ever met a payroll?   What's the percentage in worrying yourself silly   over a bunch of fool questions like

I know of a group of adults in a Presbyterian church who first read this creed with a sense of indignation and rejection. Two months later, their indignation had softened; six months later, one of their members reported, the majority conceded their general satisfaction with this creed as an expression of what they really did believe. Such a creed, they admitted, did not fit the New Testament very closely, but at least it was honest.

But a truly honest statement of belief is hard for any man to make. What do I really believe about myself, my world, my neighbors, the whole of things? Perhaps no man ever finishes his answer to such a question. Even the Christian church never finishes making up its mind about its beliefs about God, if the history of creed-making down through the ages is any indication. But from age to age religious bodies like the church do publish creeds to make clear to themselves and others what the beginning, the root, the ultimate reference of their thinking and behaving seems to be. These creeds represent "our best thoughts" on the matter, even though we know our behavior often contradicts "our best thoughts."

"Who am I?" "What am I doing here?"

I've got an answer to the one big question.

I got mine.

It is in this spirit that I have tried to state what I believe as a Christian as I begin to think about making moral judgments on issues in American economic life. (The sum total of my faith as a Christian is not written out here, but only those dimensions of the faith that seem especially significant for my thinking about moral issues in American economic life.) The hope is that this confession of faith may move readers to probe into the roots of the meaning of life for them. What any person discovers about himself in such probing will be a large influence on how he deals with issues of the economic and every other side of human life.

I believe that the visible world is the gift of the invisible Creator who made and sustains the world in his love. He is not the world, for he made it, but he is everywhere present in this world. Before any of his creatures took thought to sustain themselves, he already sustained them. All the work that the creatures do to keep themselves alive depends upon his work as their Creator. God is the giver of everything that keeps me alive, and of more besides.

I believe that the basic issue of human existence is whether love or hate is to prevail between all creatures. The great decision of my life is between the clenched fist raised against my brother and the open hand extended to him. I live in a history burdened with the fist, the ax, and the gun, and I am tempted to believe that competition, oppression, and egotism are the basic forces in human life. But I believe in the judgment of the creation by its Creator, who also sustains it through his unrelenting condemnation of all that denies his love.

I believe that the judgment and the love of our Creator came into this world visibly in the person of Jesus of Nazareth, whose presence in our history assures us that nothing shall separate us from the love of God. He entered into the common economic life of men as a carpenter. He undertook the uncommon task of preaching the good news of God's love for the poor. He endured the hostility of the world in order to defeat that hostility and to install in all human affairs the power of the love of God.

I believe in the Spirit who raised Jesus from the dead, who stirs us men to hope for the coming of the kingdom of God, who confirms our faith that this world is wholly subject to his will, and who constantly renews in the lives of the faithful their will and capacity to have compassion on their fellow creatures.

I believe that man does not live by bread alone, but that the giving and receiving of bread is an occasion for acknowledging the love of God. I believe that no earthly power, no system, no inventions of man are immune to the measuring judgment and the saving grace of God. I believe that he is at work in the world, bringing hope to the poor, rebuke to the rich, and the increase of caring among all men. And because he surely works for such purposes, I commit myself to work with him, to the same purposes, so long as I shall live.

Questions for Further Reflection

1. If you agree that our moral judgments are shaped ultimately by our personal faith, do we have the right to criticize the moral decisions of other people who have based *their* decisions upon *their* own faith? In other words, what right do we have to expect other men to share and live by the moral judgments that *we* make in light of *our* beliefs?

2. A nation expresses its moral judgments through

laws, policies, traditions, customs. Look at some current federal laws or policies—e.g., the income tax, desegregation requirements, "truth-in-lending" regulations. What moral judgments do these express? What is the source or bases of these judgments?

3. Is "representative democracy" or "majority rule" a satisfactory means for deciding questions of morality? Why or why not?

3 | MONEY:
My Master or God's Servant?

We have said that the purpose of these pages is to help readers do their own digging-up of their assumptions, their presuppositions, about their economic affairs; to identify what contribution the Christian faith may make to these assumptions; and to prepare the reader thereby to define for himself ethical behavior in the realm of economic relationships.

How can anything written on a page help any man do that? That is quite a question, and no writer rests easily with his answer to it. The real test of book-reading is what goes on in the reader's own mind, and the best books I have read are the ones that strike up a real conversation between my mind and the writer's.

Any book on ethics is especially conducive to conversation, for two reasons. One, ethical issues usually involve relationships between two or more people. Two, making ethical judgments also involves fitting one thing (like some conviction about the right or good thing to do) to another thing (a human situation like a budget), and deciding on the *right fit* may further involve a sort of inner conversation in one's own mind. Some people regard talking with yourself as the sign of a mental problem. I suspect that it is very normal, especially when people are trying to "make up their minds" about a decision.

To make up our minds on a subject as complicated as moral issues in the American economy, the conversational process is exceedingly necessary. Much of the rest of this study, therefore, will contain actual conversations concerning such issues. They were carried on by several groups generous enough to spend a series of evenings in early 1971 talking with me and each other about these issues.

Both variety and uniformity mark these particular people. All were Americans, all were of the white race, most were between the ages of thirty and fifty, all were middle class, and all had some "stake" in the economy of the United States. They were asked to participate in order to help write this book, and the particular persons were chosen because something in their background—usually their job—gave them some insights into the moral and economic issues of American life.[3]

Every reader will recognize that the American economy has many people like these in its assorted sectors:

David Kendrick, an agent for a national insurance company.

Tom Merrill, a research electronics engineer with a large national corporation.

Ann Merrill, his wife, who is active in community affairs, the church, and politics.

Ralph Lewis, a university mathematics professor and an elder in the Presbyterian church.

Margaret Lewis, his wife, who is a public school teacher and a deacon in the church.

This first conversation began to come to a focus when one person in the group asked: Do "ethical issues" arise chiefly in the lives of individual persons, or do they arise just as much in institutions? The relative importance of, and the relation between, personal and institutional ethics became one of the major issues of the evening. In and around this issue were woven versions of another question: are there Christian guidelines for the management of money, personally or institutionally?

KENDRICK: I don't want to hold up my industry—insurance —as a model, but I'm rather proud of the medical insurance for over-65 people that we have recently set up. Many insurance companies, you know, cancel medical insurance on people when they reach age sixty-five. These insurance companies have "left the customer" much as the railroads left their passengers.

LEWIS: You've got another problem in the insurance companies now, since the federal government let them deal in common stocks.

MERRILL: What's wrong with that?

LEWIS: Nothing unless you sell in such blocks that you disturb the market.

MERRILL: Do you blame the insurance companies or the brokerage system?

LEWIS: I blame the system, but the greatest offenders are insurance companies *and* educational foundations; I don't blame your business any more than mine! When Harvard University decides to unload 200,000 shares of Chrysler, *things happen* on the market, whether they want it to or not.

MERRILL: I don't think you can criticize anyone for selling while stocks are on the downtrend just because that will reinforce the downtrend. You can't criticize insurance companies or anyone for using their power, unless they are doing it unethically.

LEWIS: Any time power is used, one is open to ethical criticism.

MERRILL: How *are* they using that power?

LEWIS: Right now many are apparently ignoring what the effect of their action may be on the economy as a whole.

SHRIVER: Yes, until a recent article in the paper, I didn't

realize that the University of North Carolina owns various chunks of stock in major corporations, including General Motors. Not long ago Ralph Nader's bunch canvassed the stock-owning universities of the country and asked them to vote with the Nader people in the G.M. stockholder meeting for some environmentally oriented changes of policy in the corporation, such as the addition of a consumer representative on the G.M. Board of Directors. The University trusts a state bank to cast its vote in the various companies in which it holds stock. In this case the university president said that it did not behoove the university to be involved in partisan political affairs. The bank usually casts its votes with management, as it did in this case. It has power put in its hands by an institution which chooses to define itself as "non-political," but which is *inevitably* political in the way it exercises its power in the economic system. So what do you say to Ralph Lewis's observation that wherever you have power being used, you have a question of ethics? Isn't it true that you'll face *some* question of ethics, because inherent in the use of power is its impact upon people whose interests it affects?

KENDRICK: In that connection, look at what the insurance companies have recently done to commit eight billion dollars to the cause of better housing in the urban ghettoes. That's a new departure for the use of investment funds for these companies. This is on the ethical "plus" side, just as the neglect of the over-65 medical insurance is on the ethical "minus" side for the insurance industry. I'd reserve the right to defend the insurance industry and throw rocks at it too! The use of investment funds to help ghetto housing impresses me as a responsible, ethical use of money.

SHRIVER: Yes. It's interesting that this money invested by insurance companies is money customers have paid for future benefits. But in the meantime, the company uses this money, under legal limits, to make money, presumably both for the company and the customer. And the question of the responsible use of money held "in trust" faces almost every large institution in our society—including the church.

For example, I wonder why in the Presbyterian Church, U.S., we do not consider using ministerial retirement funds (which now amount to about ninety million dollars), or a portion of such funds, in ways that will be beneficial to society, rather than investing it all on the principle of "maximum protection of the investor"?

ANN M.: I can give you a perfect example of that. In a town in this country, the local OEO program has set up a credit union which now gives 5 percent return. It's regulated and protected by the government, but this credit union needs some investors who can put in more than the five dollars a month that is the maximum for many poor people in the town. These are the people who want to be able to borrow money that they cannot borrow through the banks.

SHRIVER: Should our churches put some of their funds in that credit union, rather than in 6 percent bonds or some other "safe" investment?

MERRILL: If you are talking about risk funds, that's all right, but if I were the administrator of the ministers' retirement fund, I would feel pretty responsible for how that money was protected.

SHRIVER: But take the difference between investing in corporate bonds, guaranteeing 6 percent, and investing in a government-guaranteed credit union for the poor at 5 percent. Might not that sacrifice in return be well worth it for the sake of what the churches like to call righteousness?

MERRILL: Who is going to lose that percentage point of interest?

SHRIVER: I am—ministers like myself.

MERRILL: How many of you are ready to do that? This is

what the fund's administrator has to know. It's a question of whose interests are primary in the management of this money. And that raises the question of on what basis you choose one interest over another. On what basis does the administrator work?

SHRIVER: His basis is presumably the basis on which everyone in the Christian church lives—the Christian basis. And it's not enough to ask, "What would Jesus do?" After all, who can answer the question, "What would Jesus do if he were the administrator of a ninety million dollar retirement fund?" A better question might be: "How, given my particular power to affect other people, can I show love for my neighbors? and more neighbors rather than fewer neighbors? and my more needy neighbors in particular?" This also requires me to answer the question, "To whom am I responsible?" And for the Christian, that question is never adequately answered in terms of a limited group of people like "my stockholders."

MERRILL: Boy, that's a tough one!

KENDRICK: Looking at it very legalistically, a trusteeship is vested with the guardianship of that money. Although you may feel benevolent, what about this minister off in the country who is nervous about his income for next year? Would he appreciate an almost 20 percent drop in his earnings—which is what a drop from 6 percent to 5 percent return would mean?

SHRIVER: Yes, for all I know, he might be legally justified in suing the Ministers' Fund for the loss. But we're raising here the question of the possible tension or even contradiction between what is right legally in our society, what is customary, and what is right ethically from the perspective of the Christian faith.

FOR REFLECTION

From time to time in our dialogues, we will break in with some suggestions for the reader's reflection on the progress of the conversation. This procedure may make it a little clearer that the point of this study is to help you, the reader, be a participant in these conversations.

Many of the basic issues to recur in later parts of this study have already surfaced in this first twenty minutes of talk among these six people. Notice the following issues:

1. What is a *just use* of money? Every person in the room that night assumed that the use of money is subject to some kind of judgment about good and bad, right and wrong. That is, spending money involves questions of ethics. Notice how often the question comes down to: "In whose interests should one's own money be spent?"

The suggestion here is that self-interest, while not to be eliminated as a consideration, is too narrow an answer. If a man says that he is making an investment on behalf of his *family's* future, we are likely to credit him with a somewhat higher ethical motive than if he were investing on behalf of himself, to the neglect of his family. "Other people's needs have some claim on 'my' money," is the unspoken "rule" assumed here. (This amounts to a rejection of a rule that some advocates of an Adam Smith-style economic philosophy would urge: "Let each man pursue his own selfish interests, and the interests of all will be served best." It is not this automatic and easy, our friends above seem to say.)

2. Whose interests, other than my own, have *primary* claim on my use of money? It is a striking fact that when Kendrick assesses the "ethical pluses and minuses" of his own industry, he is concerned with recent company actions towards two groups of people, the elderly and the ghetto-dweller. These two are similar in that they tend to be

among the groups in our society with the lowest incomes.
Why should Kendrick, and one or two others, be so
sensitive to actions related to the poor?

His personal answer to this question does not come
out here, but Shriver's answer does come out. He poses
a series of short inquiries that tell us something of the
general standards he tends to apply in making moral judgments about economic issues: How can I show love for my
neighbors? more neighbors rather than fewer? my neediest
neighbors in particular?

This is an attempt to summarize a sort of checklist
of concepts basic to one approach to ethics—the approach
of Christians. Love of God and neighbor is the "sum"
of ethics in the Christian perspective. Such love the Christian sees in Jesus. Such love reaches out to help the
"neighbor"—the man near at hand. In turn, Christian love
puts no limits on the human "neighborhood," which means
that every man is my neighbor, a potential claimant upon
my service.

But, as the ministry of Jesus strongly suggests, real
love is expressed to particular persons. And sometimes,
with our limited time, energy, and other resources, every
one of us must choose to be helpers to some of our neighbors rather than others. Who should those neighbors be?
If Jesus' story of the good Samaritan is a clue, the answer
is: the man most in need, the man at the bottom of the
ladder, the injured man on the roadside.

This same concern will be expressed many other
times in this study by Christians. However, the question,
"To whom am I primarily responsible in the management
of my money?" cannot be answered with the help of
merely this one rule or norm. Already in this dialogue
Merrill has said that funds given "in trust" for certain

purposes should be used by the trust fund administrator in ways consistent with the desires of those who set up the fund. The norm here might be roughly translated: "Live up to your agreements, your covenants, your contracts."

But there is obviously a problem here. In a society that requires us all on occasion to make an accounting for money put into our hands by other people for certain purposes, what can be done about our obligations to the poor? The poor make few contracts regarding retirement funds, for they don't have the money to invest in such funds. Here is the beginning of a vicious economic circle: the less money you have, the less you are going to have. And the beginning of an ethical conflict: one's obligation to "the have's" frustrates one's obligation to "the have not's."

3. What is the *relative importance* of economic, legal, and ethical "rules"? The people in our conversation show their sensitivity to a variety of guidelines for behavior that might be lumped together as "rules." "As a rule," we say, "one expects to get a return of interest on money he is saving"—though our Genevan merchant in chapter 1 reminds us that only in the past five hundred years have Westerners accepted this *economic rule* without dispute.

But how much interest should it earn? "As much or as little as the market allows," some will answer. "Not in some instances," the American government now says. "We have some *legal rules* against charging too much interest on money (such as 36 percent on installment purchases) and some legal rules against trust fund executives making risky investments of trust funds."

Finally, the inclination of Christians moves them

to talk about yet another kind of rule, a *moral rule*: "We must operate our economic system with special concern for how it affects poor people."

How are we to weigh the *relative claims* of these several sorts of rules? You can tell a lot about any person's general approach to judgment-making on economic issues by his way of answering this question. Consider the following three possible positions:

> Economic systems have their own laws; legal and moral rules are just plain interference with something that works best when left alone. (The radical free-enterpriser)

> The government should regulate the economy at all points to insure just distribution of goods. (The radical socialist)

> I intend to do the right thing even if it conflicts with

Loose spending
has to stop.

We're bled dry
by taxes.

Operating costs
are up.

what political and economic systems tell us to do.
(The radical moralist)

Most people—including those in this conversation—
refuse to take any one of these radical positions. They
want to have their behavior influenced by all three sorts
of rules. But the three do not easily blend together in
decision-making. How much interest is too much or too
little on church workers' retirement funds? How much
justice must be done to the needs of investors, the needs
of the poor, the laws of one's country, the laws of the
economic system? No easy thing to decide! But often in
digging into economic issues, it turns out that decisions
have to be made in terms of *the relative weight one is
ready to give these several sorts of rules.* We shall have
many occasions in the rest of this study to take note of
this subtlety, as the rest of this very dialogue will illus-
trate.

Why, it costs us
thousands each year
for lobbyists just to
maintain our defense
contracts.

It would be nice to
help the poor in our
own country and the
world

but we must
be fiscally
responsible.

PART II

MARGARET L.: I should think that the fund's administrator has
   a responsibility to his stockholders to protect their future
   retirement.

SHRIVER: Yes, but let's remember we've already assumed that
   we are going to invest the funds in the economic system
   of the country, that we are not going to sew the money
   up in a mattress or bury it (as one man did—Luke
   19:11ff.). And we invest this money, with reasonable
   safety, in order to serve the interests of those who put the
   money in the fund. My question is: is the definition of
   responsibility *wide* enough if we restrict it merely to
   those who have put the money in? That delivers the
   "investment judgment" from having to reckon with anybody else's interests but those who have invested the
   money. Then the church as an investor uses exactly the
   same set of justifications as is used by any business corporation. D. T. Jenkins said once that "the church is
   as secular as any other institution," and I think that he
   is right, if our discussion is any indication.

MERRILL: The fact that you are investing in a retirement
   fund means that you want some sort of security for your
   old age. That's a particular purpose you have in mind.
   A minister presumably could invest his money in something else, and the administrator of that fund would have
   some other responsibility.

LEWIS: Yes, I would say that a church board of missions
   would have greater freedom and reason to invest in a
   small town credit union for the poor. Funds could be
   given to that board for such purposes.

SHRIVER: Yes, I admit that may be a better procedure. But
   it should be pointed out in all this how solicitous we
   tend to be concerning "my retirement funds" and a
   maximum buildup of such funds, when none of us, including myself, has proposed a *radical risk* of those funds.
   For example, all I have proposed for a more "righteous"

use of my retirement fund is a use that may decrease its investment return by a percentage point of interest. If I got less than 4 percent growth annually, I would probably get a little worried. And if the principal began to decline, I would get more than a little worried.

We live in an economic system that has assumed for some 500 years that "It's wrong to keep good money idle," and Christians long ago made peace with the idea of renting out money for a charge. All we're arguing about is whether a Christian, charged by his faith with a particular concern for poor people, should be willing to make a modest "sacrifice" out of deference to that concern. We're not talking about *much* sacrifice by New Testament standards; it's embarrassingly little, as a matter of fact. And it would seem that the insurance companies who have put their billions in ghetto housing are open to at least as much reduction of investment earnings as the church is open to.

KENDRICK: Of course, you could say that the insurance companies acted because they were under political pressure to do so.

SHRIVER: In terms of ethical results, of course, that may be irrelevant, unless one decides that one's motive in doing a thing, rather than the results of the action, is the real touchstone of his ethics.

KENDRICK: Well, it's a matter of mutual benefit all around, at any rate. The company still has hope for some gain, even though investment in low-cost housing may not be the most profitable possible investment.

ANN M.: Yes, and maybe it is a hope for a *long* term gain for the company and all of us in this country. If the cities collapse and become unlivable, we all are the losers. To desire a long term gain for more people than your own stockholders would be a responsible ethical action in any area of business activity, I should think.

MERRILL: Another point: doesn't the very security of your

retirement income give you additional freedom to give to the poor some of your income right now?

SHRIVER: Yes, that's a good point. I can work on the same Christian basis if I treat one portion of my income as inviolate retirement money, and another portion as "risk capital" on behalf of the poor. I might then even free myself to risk more of my total income for such a purpose than a niggardly 1 or 2 percent of interest points on retirement funds. But all this close calculation still makes me uncomfortable as someone who at least claims to be a follower of Jesus Christ. How does all this discussion sound when some other followers of Jesus in the New Testament were told to leave everything and follow him (Luke 18:18 ff.)?

KENDRICK: It goes back to one's sense of values, I guess. We seem to be asking, where in the budget of the individual lies his responsibility to the needy people of the society? It also brings us back to our own *self-satisfaction* in spending money. The whole monetary problem comes back to the individual, his sense of what's important, his values, you might say.

ANN M.: Whether you are willing to give much to the poor is partly a matter of whether you were raised to take a good income for granted, isn't it? You can pay a lot more attention to spending money, when you are sure that you are making enough.

LEWIS: Well, as for the man who sells everything and lives the hermit life, I think some people are called to this. But other people are called to administer wealth and to be sensitive and to have concern for others. It's *hard* for a rich man to get into heaven, but it's not impossible; he does not necessarily give it all away, but he uses it with sensitivity and concern, whatever that means! I dislike the idea of giving up everything to live a life of poverty. It might be all right for some people, but others are called to the sensitive use of money, which involves having to *fight* constantly in yourself, for you are always better off than somebody else.

SHRIVER: Giving it all away does not appear to be the only Christian option; Jesus did not demand this of everybody he met. But it does mean something to everybody to say that God is the giver of all wealth and still has some rightful say about how wealth is managed.

LEWIS: Plus the fact that when my money occupies a position that desensitizes me to the needs of other people, I find myself in exactly the same position as the rich man. In fact, sometimes I *am* that rich man. And Jesus is right there, waiting to know what I am going to do with his invitation, "Follow me." Here I am, golf clubs, swimming pool, automobile, and all, and he is asking me to be his disciple.... It puts us all in a tough spot, doesn't it?

Postscript

It does indeed . . . especially if "all of us" means "all of us Christians." Obviously one could avoid many a "tough spot" of decision-making if one were willing to eliminate from one's mind "the upward call of God in Christ Jesus" (Phil. 3:14).

Genuine differences have existed among Christians from early times over the application of this "upward call" to the Christian's relationship to his own possessions. A literal obedience to Jesus' command to the rich young ruler has during almost twenty centuries sent thousands of churchmen into the monastery. But as Ralph Lewis rightly points out in his comments above, there are other ways of fulfilling responsibility for neighbors. One remembers how Leo Tolstoy, who owned a large estate in nineteenth century Russia, made a vow to live a life of poverty and spiritual meditation. Then one day a serf was accidentally killed, partly because Tolstoy had neglected his duties as administrator of his estate. What is one's duty if he happens to have sizable economic resources at his command? What is one's duty if, as an American, he lives in the richest country in the history of the world? Are we called to give it all up for the poor? to give some of it up? to manage all of it more ethically?

The next two chapters of our study will explore these latter questions at some length. Meantime, Ralph Lewis's observation is worth repeating to every reader of these pages who wants to call himself a Christian: "Sometimes I am that rich man. And Jesus is right there, waiting to know what I am going to do with his invitation, 'Follow me.' "

Questions for Further Reflection

1. Ann M. stated, "To desire a long term gain for more people than your own stockholders would be a responsible ethical action in any area of business activity, I should think." Do you think most corporations presently operate on that basis? Support your answer, giving examples of corporate activities and policies.

2. Vast amounts of our "investment monies" go into government at local, state, and national levels. Do we have a responsibility for how that money is managed? If so, what guidelines and/or moral principles do we have as Christians and citizens which indicate how that money should be used?

4 | COMPETITION:
Does It Build or Destroy?

The next conversational group to appear here was composed primarily of businessmen who were presidents of their corporations or managers of their local manufacturing plants. Two members of the group were theologians.

That we should continue our deliberating about ethical issues in the American economy by eavesdropping on a conversation between businessmen and theologians is rather appropriate. Almost any historian would say that for the past two hundred years the history of America could not possibly be understood without reference to two great American "types," the businessman and the Protestant. Some would even say that the spirit of the hardworking businessman and the spirit of the individualistic, morally intense Protestant go hand and hand in traditional American culture.

Most American businessmen and theologians are well enough informed about the issues of their own national economy to know that these issues are intertwined with issues of worldwide importance. America is now a world power as never before in history, and it is a world power politically, militarily, *and* economically.

In recognition of this, previous to the following discussion the six participants read some paragraphs from the eloquent pen of another geographical variety of American—a Latin American named Ivan Illich. This former Roman Catholic priest, now the director of the

Center for Intercultural Documentation in Cuernavaca, Mexico, identifies the ethical issues of North and South American economies from the standpoint of one who looks at the competitive, industrial production system of the North and finds it lacking in services for people who live in the South. Since "the American economy" is sometimes summarily equated with "the competitive free enterprise system," it seemed on target to preface our thinking that evening with a reading of the following passage by Illich, as a way to begin an exploration of the *ethical and economic ramifications of competition.* (Actually this quotation helps set the stage for both chapters 4 and 5 of this study.)

OUTWITTING THE "DEVELOPED" COUNTRIES[4]

Ivan Illich

. . . Factories, news media, hospitals, governments, and schools produce goods and services packaged to contain our view of the world. We—the rich— conceive of progress as the expansion of these establishments. We conceive of heightened mobility as luxury and safety packaged by General Motors or Boeing. We conceive of improving the general well-being as increasing the supply of doctors and hospitals, which package health along with protracted suffering. We have come to identify our need for further learning with the demand for ever-longer confinement to classrooms. In other words, we have packaged education with custodial care, certification for jobs, and the right to vote, and wrapped them all together with indoctrination in the Christian, liberal, or Communist virtues.

In less than a hundred years industrial society

has molded patent solutions to basic human needs and converted us to the belief that man's needs were shaped by the Creator as demands for the products we have invented. This is as true for Russia and Japan as for the North Atlantic community. The consumer is trained for obsolescence, which means continuing loyalty toward the same producers who will give him the same basic packages in different quality or new wrappings.

*   *   *

Each car which Brazil puts on the road denies fifty people good transportation by bus. Each merchandised refrigerator reduces the chance of building a community freezer. Every dollar spent in Latin America on doctors and hospitals costs a hundred lives, to adopt a phrase of Jorge de Ahumada, the brilliant Chilean economist. Had each dollar been spent on providing safe drinking water, a hundred lives could have been saved. Each dollar spent on schooling means more privileges for the few at the cost of the many; at best it increases the number of those who, before dropping out, have been taught that those who stay longer have earned the right to more power, wealth, and prestige. What such schooling does is to teach the schooled the superiority of the better schooled.

*   *   *

Continued technological refinements of products which are already established on the market frequently benefit the producer far more than the consumer. The more complex production processes tend to enable only the largest producer continually to replace outmoded models, and to focus the demand of the consumer on the marginal improvement of what he buys, no matter what the concomitant side effects: higher prices, diminished life-span, less general usefulness, higher cost of repairs. Think of the multiple uses for a simple can opener, whereas an electric one, if it works at all, opens only some kinds of cans, and costs one hundred times as much.

This is equally true for a piece of agricultural machinery and for an academic degree. The Midwestern farmer can become convinced of his need for a four-axle vehicle which can go 70 mph on the highways, has an electric windshield wiper and upholstered seats, and can be turned in for a new one within a year or two. Most of the world's farmers don't need such speed, nor have they ever met with such comfort, nor are they interested in obsolescence. They need low-priced transport, in a world where time is not money, where manual wipers suffice, and where a piece of heavy equipment should outlast a generation. Such a mechanical donkey requires entirely different engineering and design than one produced for the U.S. market. This vehicle is not in production.

Participants in the conversation to follow are:

John Delaney: Manager of the local plant of a large national corporation specializing in the manufacture of heavy metal equipment. The local plant employs some 250 persons. Delaney, in his mid-thirties, has been rapidly promoted in the national corporation.

Philip Keller: President of a corporation which produces agricultural and food product processing equipment for a national and international market. By profession he is an engineer. Three plants are located in the United States, one in South America.

Carl Everett: President and founder of a small equipment business. He is an elder in his local Presbyterian church.

Art McCrary: Professor of Christian Education and Nurture in a nearby university theological school, concerned for many years about the relation of Christian theology to the work world of the businessman.

These particular men have participated on previous occasions in discussions like the one recorded below. The tone of the dialogue, therefore, is probably more forthright than might otherwise be expected.

*   *   *

SHRIVER: Ivan Illich in his writings makes many specific criticisms of the North American's economic relations with South Americans, but one of his key general criticisms of our economic system is of the bad effects of *competition,* which is so prominent a feature of our industrial system. He also criticizes, by implication, the individual "get ahead" spirit of the South American middle class, who in his view resemble too much the North American middle class. He raises the whole issue of competition and its relation to human welfare. It's an ethical issue for him, as it has been for other Christians. What about competition—is it just a fact of life, is it a threat to human welfare, or is it of great human benefit?

KELLER: First off I would say that the discipline of competition is needed by many human beings to insure their performance. Within the realm of education, for example, my son tells me that during this last term at college one of his professors was more absent than present in meetings of his classes. Here is a "free agent" who presumably loves the subject for its own sake but nobody is regulating him. There has to be a regulatory agency in society to discipline individual and group performance. Competition is such a regulatory device.

DELANEY: Furthermore, one is not always competing against someone else. My strongest competitor is *me*. My last performance in a given circumstance is the bench mark I want to exceed the next time around. It's my carrot, my standard of value.

Also, in any enterprise—education, business, government—standards of value must be set. For example, if I were on trial for my life, I would want the best lawyer in the field. I would want to know who was the best, and I would hope that the law schools and the law profession would have standards of individual performance that would help me find the best. I don't want a lawyer who got much personal benefit from law school but who got so many F's that he barely graduated! All men should have some reward in life, all right, but the competitive norm is necessary for the benefit of people like myself, who may need superior service and who must have some measure of superiority.

SHRIVER: On the other hand, is it possible to think of a human group which has high standards of achievement but which does not choose to *rank-order* its members' individual degree of meeting those standards? For example, would it be good or bad to announce at the beginning of an academic course that everybody in the class *could* get an "A," that the number of A's would not be arbitrarily limited? You could say that without abandoning some standards for measuring "A" performance.

EVERETT: If you were going to announce that, you shouldn't give grades at all!

DELANEY: How can anyone know just where he stands unless he sometimes looks back and sees where the rest of the pack is?

SHRIVER: That's just the issue! Should one relate to the "pack" of other human beings as though we were all in a race or as though we were all lifting some weight that required everybody's strength? Is there some real value in rank-ordering among human beings? Or does the habit of rank-ordering have its "dehumanizing" aspects? In many areas of human life, at least, competition and rank-ordering are apparently *not* the preferable accent for human relationships. Among my children, I see a little too much competition. I do not have often to choose among my friends a "best" friend. And with some of my work associates what we achieve individually is partly a function of how well we collaborate.

DELANEY: You're suggesting that we could have a "zero-defects" standard which a lot of people in a group might actually achieve?

SHRIVER: Yes, and in your industrial production setting, the "zero-defects" goal for the organization requires the cooperation of every single member of your work force. There are some activities in your plant in which you don't want your people to consider themselves competitors. A safety record, for example, is something that everybody helps compile. An "A" grade is given to the plant organization as a whole for so many days without an accident.

DELANEY: That's true, and I would like to think that the job

Why do we do this to ourselves?   Why are we in this rat race?

of management is to direct the competitive spirit towards one's industrial competitors in the market. That would mean fostering cooperation within the group for competition with other groups. Management's job is like that of the coach of the Baltimore Colts—the left and right tackles are competitors, all right, but he wants them to work as a team against the Dallas Cowboys.

SHRIVER: That gets us to the question of "internal" versus "external" motivations for action, doesn't it? Take the case of the successes of America's Apollo missions to the moon. Did Americans make it to the moon first out of competition with Russia or out of some remarkable cooperation between government, industry, and thousands of skilled people in this country? Did these people succeed mostly because they had a "beat the Russians" attitude, or because the "carrot" of an unprecedented human achievement lured them on, and made them want to collaborate? Isn't the beat-somebody motive inferior to the let's-achieve-something-together motivation? And wouldn't the moon-landing have been even more splendid as a human achievement if we had done it *with* the Russians?

KELLER: Don't forget that in this massive space program in the United States, there was competition at every step of the way. Remember the cartoon on the two astronauts? They are out there in space, and one turns to

I can't speak for you . . .

But I think it's the money!

the other and says, "Just think, there are 12,000 parts in this capsule, every one built by the low bidder!"

McCrary: The least we can say is that a great variety of motivations was present. What may have motivated Congress to appropriate the money—to beat the Russians—probably did not motivate scientists and astronauts; they valued the achievement in itself.

Keller: Yes, you can be sure that for the industries involved the competition was intense to supply the right parts, at the right price, at the right time. There was money to be made from these contracts, but not every company wanting that money was able to make good competitively on its contract bids. That's one way we got excellence in the equipment. And it's the way we got thousands of people in hundreds of companies to hustle, to exert a lot of effort. Few of them may have thought much about the Russians. They did think about the money, and competition for that was strong all down the line. In fact, I agree that competition is woven into the very fabric of our being.

Shriver: That is the basic question, I guess. *Is* competition woven into the fabric of our being? Is it part of being a "good man" to be a "good competitor"?

Delaney: Perhaps the element of cooperation and the element of competition are *both* woven into our being and are not mutually exclusive. The competitive spirit can be fulfilled in cooperation. Take *war* for example—intense cooperation among some people for intense competition with others. It's important, I should think, to know when competition is foolish and when it is necessary. One could even say that the self-preservation of the whole human race is a necessary goal for man, and competition to reach *that* goal would be a very high-minded sort of competition!

Shriver: It would indeed. Not many nations in the world give strong evidence of competing for such a goal, though one could say that whenever nations get together to talk about the limitation of nuclear weapon production, or about saving the world's oceans from pollution, they are basically concerned about such a goal. The human race's current vulnerability to self-destruction calls for some identification of mutual interests all around the globe, does it not? In this connection the Christian faith apparently holds out a high but very practical hope: that men may be converted to the love of their neighbors "as themselves." Such love puts the self and the neighbor together in one fellowship, wherein the question, "Who's the winner?" is not even relevant.

McCrary: The Christian faith does assume that it takes some converting, that the competitive motive is still very real. It's a matter of how the two views are evaluated in light of the faith. It's a question, too, of how capable we are of "enlightened self-interest," and whether on occasion the *sacrifice* of one person's interest to another's is ethically called for.

Delaney: So that we must say that the more competitive you are, the less Christian you are?

Shriver: It would be an error to reduce the principle of "love your neighbor" to that form. Perhaps I am saying that competition may be one necessary relationship among men as an expression of the discipline of standards of excellence, but that the competitive spirit needs the discipline of a love that is essentially noncompetitive.

Delaney: I couldn't disagree more. I can be extremely competitive on a variety of levels with any human being and still have the deepest respect and love for that individual. I have *nothing* against my largest competitor in business. I don't know him personally, of course, but I enjoy the competition involved when I read *The Wall Street Journal* and see that I earned more per share than he did! That's the value judgment that my peer group is putting on my performance versus my competitor's.

Shriver: And if you put them out of business because of your superior performance, what do you think about that?

DELANEY: That's not my goal.

SHRIVER: No, but suppose it's a consequence of pursuing your goal?

DELANEY: I would feel that *I* had lost something: my source of external competition against which to measure my success. It would be like losing the opposing team you're playing ball with.

SHRIVER: Anywhere in your strategies, your policies, your activities as an industrialist, would you have some concern for the effects your superior performance may have on people whose performance you exceed?

DELANEY: I'd know going out of business is a tough experience. But I'm not sure I would know what to do about my competitor's problem there.

KELLER: It's not a matter of "hating your competitor." It's like four men playing golf together every week, who compete fiercely but who have great affection for each other.

FOR REFLECTION

Competition is a tricky subject to discuss. It is evidently an "iffy" subject, too. Already the discussion above suggests that competition might be a *good* thing *if and when:*

—it protects people from yielding to the temptation of doing sloppily a job worth doing well;

—it encourages one group (such as producers) to do the best possible work for another group (such as consumers);

—it helps individual human beings develop all of their talents.

And the discussion suggests that competition might be a *bad* thing *if and when:*

—it hinders people from recognizing that a given achievement calls for cooperation;

—it discourages some from doing their best work because of their prior certainty that they are usually "losers";

"Everyone for himself," the elephant said dancing among the ants.

—it tempts winners to deny responsibility for what happens to losers;

—the conditions of competition are unequal. ("Everyone for himself," the elephant said, dancing among the ants.)

The next portions of the dialogue will suggest strongly that competition is a good thing in its place (on the football field, keeping prices down) but a bad thing out of its place (in families, in the relations of very rich and very poor people); therefore competition must be hedged in by the "discipline" of *other* considerations that make a man or a society worthy of being called "good." For now it is worth observing that no one in the discussion so far was willing to *equate* "good man" and "good competitor."

To this may be added a further personal observation: Shriver's suggestion that a "no-grade" policy might be used in the academic classroom is a response in part to students on college campuses who are saying to their professors these days: "All through the public school system we were graded, compared, and put into categories. We're tired of having our status as human beings linked to our 'standing' in a class of other human beings! It's time in America that we got over our image of life as a great race to 'sucess' in which some win, some lose. Let's build a society in which *everyone is a winner*." Something like an American cultural revolution is reflected in statements like these. Such statements suggest the hope that society will more and more show the value of every one of its members and less and less insist on men knowing their value in comparison with each other.

Young people's apparent demotion of competition as a virtue may puzzle older Americans. Ours has been a highly competitive society from early in our history, especially in the economic realm. Many factors in modern American life, however, make young people aware of the limits of competition as a constructive human relationship. They see parents and other adults acquire ulcers and assorted frustrations over the "rat race" in their daily work. They look at social problems like racism and war, and they conclude that men's tendency to find reasons for deeming themselves superior to other men is destructive. They see so many of the world's current problems involving competition between men for morally shabby prizes— e.g. prestige and power—that they are suspicious of the worth of competition, whether or not it is "woven into the fabric of our being."

From an ethical and religious perspective the competitive urge could be ever so real a "fact" of human nature and still be an urge that should be put under the control of urges believed to be higher. That is the point of view taken by the anthropologist Loren Eiseley, who says that Charles Darwin and Thomas Huxley overestimated the survival value of competition between species and between members of the same species. The only reason that some biological species have survived is that in the long history of evolution their members *have learned to cooperate* with each other, and of no species is this truer, says Eiseley, than of man.

> Man's altruistic and innately co-operative character has brought him along the road to civilization far more than the qualities of the ape and tiger . . .
>
> Today we know that early man was small and scant in numbers and that most of his efforts must have been given over to food-getting rather than conflict. This is not to minimize his destructive qualities, but his long-drawn-out, helpless childhood,

during which his growing brain matured, could only have flourished in the safety of a stable family organization—groups marked by altruistic and long-continued care of the young.[5]

Eiseley goes on to point out that some of the earliest known human graves in Africa have in them skeletons of cripples who were apparently cared for by their tribe for long years after injury had rendered them unproductive. In this view, what any human tribe does about its "losers" is a singular mark of its evolutionary success. Eiseley is making a moral judgment on the matter: the superior human being is the one who has learned to love his neighbor. In this, the anthropologist is agreeing with the New Testament.

PART II
Rules for the Struggle: The Dialogue Resumed

That there are *some* benefits and *some* dangers in the competitive urge, in economic and other affairs, is fair to conclude from the dialogue earlier in this chapter. How to get the benefits and protect against the dangers are the twin issues that the dialogue next picks up. We broke off above amidst the discussion of the difficulty of combining "fierce competition" with "great affection." To effect such a combination is the aim of certain regulations that society adopts from time to time to control competition between its members in certain ways. "Keeping the competitive urge within bounds," and the nature of those boundaries, became the center of attention for a while in our conversation. Shriver compared economic competition to a game of football.

SHRIVER: The rule against clipping, for example, is designed to protect the players against certain serious injuries.

Other rules help insure a game in which players can compete for victory without, say, killing each other. People do get killed in football, but the rules try to eliminate that. Some sports, like bullfighting and boxing, have become morally questionable in many people's minds just because it seems impossible to provide such competition under any set of rules that will sufficiently protect human life.

If one examines the American business system, one would probably find that it has some equivalents of rules and regulations that express, sometimes only vaguely, a moral concern for people who might otherwise be hurt by the working of the competitive system. Child labor laws and antitrust laws are two examples.

DELANEY: Yes, businessmen are conscious almost every day of having some rules to follow in their effort to compete in the marketplace. For example, I can't buy out my competitor if it will result in restraining trade. I can't steal his patents or do anything to endanger his right to compete with me.

MCCRARY: Such rules are not intrinsic to the competitive process, I gather. They are imposed, so to speak, from outside for the sake of certain values that the competitors or their regulators agree must be preserved.

KELLER: Think too of all the government regulations you must adhere to if you employ more than six or eight people. Insurance, social security, unemployment compensation payments, minimum wages, nondiscriminatory employment, salary continuation schemes, and regular inspections are all part of the system of rules designed to protect various people.

EVERETT: But with all this, there is still a case to be made for letting a given company go out of business as the penalty for not making productive use of the scarce resources of the country. If he can't efficiently use the resources, he ought to go out of business. It will be best for him to fold up shop.

SHRIVER: Best for him, or best for consumers who get, say, better products at better prices from other producers?

EVERETT: Maybe even best for him. I think about the little town of Enterprise, Alabama, which has in its town square a monument honoring the boll weevil. The weevil came some years ago and wiped out the cotton crop. So they switched to peanuts and achieved a surer economic footing as a result. In the short range, it looked like disaster, but in a longer range it turned out to be their economic salvation.

SHRIVER: Suppose you extend that sort of analysis a little further then, from cotton growing to cotton spinning and weaving, and from a particular town to all of New England, then all of America. When New England lost most of its textile industry to the South in the early twentieth century, that looked like a disaster to New Englanders. Over the last fifty years they have replaced many of their textile industries with higher-paying industries. And now textiles in the South are beginning to feel the pinch of world competition. Is it possible that the best thing that could happen to the textile industry in the South would be for it to be put out of business by foreign textiles?

EVERETT: It might be so. But my friends in the textile industry would tell you a different story!

DELANEY: The United States should not allow that to happen without efforts by government and industry to relocate, retrain, and revitalize the people dislocated by such an economic change. After all, an arbitrary protection of textiles' competitive position has been built up for years in this country, and you can't withdraw that protection without replacing it with some equal force. It may be all very well to send foreign aid to other countries so that they develop competitive industrial capacity, but in the meantime you owe it to your own people to protect them against the inevitable impact of that competition.

SHRIVER: Which suggests a national policy which looks forward to a decline in domestic textiles accompanied by the employee relocation, retraining, and resource re-allocation.

DELANEY: Basically that is what the government's policy is, though in a very haphazard fashion, from the Marshall Plan to the present. Look at what President Nixon has said to domestic steel producers about their price raises: he has threatened them with increases in our imports of Japanese steel! Think of all the interesting issues which this raises: a Japanese steel industry was built up and used to make war on us; we bombed it out; with our help they built it up again; now one of our leaders is using their steel prices to threaten our domestic steel producers. That's quite a cycle!

MCCRARY: It's somewhat bewildering, but doesn't it suggest that, even on a world scale, the competitive race for power and wealth gets balanced and controlled a bit by the use of power and wealth to serve something like the "general welfare"? In this case, the U.S. President is so concerned about inflation that he is willing to use foreign competition against a particular interest that goes against the general interest of the country. It's a haphazard way of pursuing the general welfare, but something more than uninhibited competition is at work.

DELANEY: Yes, and it serves to remind us that we don't live in a real laissez-faire world market. We are subject to restraints that intervene in many ways. Today (January 1971) my country intervenes and forbids me to trade with Red China and with Cuba, for example. That's okay by me, but I'm just pointing out that by consenting to be a member of this national society, I have given up certain rights and freedoms, including some economic freedoms. This means there are some issues of *group* action that I cannot deal with as an *individual*. The ethical question may have to be differently phrased in the two situations: you can't talk about Adam Smith-style, laissez-faire, guiding-hand competition in the world of

1971. We have political structures, trade barriers, and other forces that keep us from having anything resembling truly competitive, free-trade world market systems. The question of whether competition is a "good thing" may be quite different on a national and world scale from what the question is, say, within your classroom or my particular industry. It might be wise to keep the question of competition between individuals separate from the question of competition, say, between whole nations.

SHRIVER: Yes, just as it might be wise to separate the question "Who can produce the best textiles at the lowest world prices?" from the question "How can we avoid harm and injustice to one particular industry in our own country?" The first question is close to being a "strictly economic question." The second very much involves our perception of moral justice. It involves what we think our obligations are to people who suffer loss from the rather impersonal operation of political and economic systems.

FOR FURTHER REFLECTION

We break off this spirited conversation again to continue it in the next chapter around the issue that is just emerging in the dialogue: what are the responsibilities of the people who benefit most from economic change to people who benefit least? More generally, what is ethically required of the rich in relation to the poor?

For now, it is well to pause in retrospect upon the conversation so far to call attention to certain features of *ethical reflection* exemplified in these live exchanges between people asked to discuss "moral judgments on issues in American economic life." Note the following characteristics of the conversation so far:

1. Everyone has some idea of what is "good" for human existence, but the ideas often collide.

The five people in the above exchange share many things in common, but when pressed, each exhibits some difference from the others in the notion of what is best for human life. Two rather different approaches to the evaluation of competition are competing here: one notion (promoted by Delaney and Keller) commends to us the life of hard-won achievements by individual human beings for whom various "carrots" are spurs to further achievements. The other notion (promoted chiefly by Shriver) accentuates a particular kind of achievement: community, neighborliness, mutual care between people. Neither party, we notice, sees itself as excluding the truth of the other side, but it is clear that certain stresses, certain priorities dominate each way of thinking. *One's stress on and priority for what is ultimately good for human life is the foundation of his ethical reflection.*

2. In questions of economics, what one considers good for people may be profoundly conditioned by his own role in the economic system.

Earlier, Ivan Illich served as a representative voice of certain poor men in our world society. The two theologians served to represent in some measure certain claims about economic ethics made in the history of the church. The most positive commendation of the competitive economic system came from three successful businessmen. It will not surprise any reader that this should be the distribution of opinion. Does it also raise some skepticism about the worthwhileness of presuming to do "ethical reflection" on economic issues?

Suppose that all so-called ethical reflection is really a reflection only of one's position and self-interest in a particular economic system? Karl Marx supposed just that: what men *think* is strictly a reflex of what roles they play

in society. Can the managers of a competitive economic
system really stand back and look critically at the very
system they help superintend?

The evidence from this conversation, actually, is
mixed. None of the business managers quoted fails to say
a good word for competition, but each recognizes the
importance of built-in restraints upon the competitive
impulse in human relationships. At the same time, the
theologians recognize that competition for the pursuit of
a goal believed to benefit all the competitors would be an
acceptable form of competition. Both sides of the discussion seem to imply that no one principle, value, or
guideline supplies sufficient backup of reasoning or justification for all our actions in the economic sphere. Thus,
"act competitively" is not the major guiding principle for
one's work *inside* his plant; "cooperate with your neighbor" takes precedence there.

For example, Delaney is unwilling for the total life
of men in society to be defined in economic terms or in
economic-competition terms alone. He desires government
to protect the casualties of competition from unjust suffering, and he thinks that forces outside the business world
should help shape the business world toward greater
justice for the poor. This is evidence that he can step back
to try to judge the actual by the desirable in the very system in which he is so deeply involved in his workaday
life. *The cynic's view that men are capable of testing their
lives only by measures that serve their self-interest has a
grain of truth in it, but it is not the full story.*

3. We reason ethically from what we see but what
we see is shaped by what we prefer to see.

"If you could just see facts flat on, without that hor-
rible moral squint; with just a little common sense, you

could have been a statesman," Cardinal Wolsey says to Sir Thomas More in Robert Bolt's play *A Man for All Seasons*. A contrary view is that "the highest test of a civilization is its sense of fact." There are so many facts to be known in the world that human beings have to select some facts as more important than others. These are the facts that stand out in our minds, like mountain peaks, as sure tokens of "reality." But by standing out in our minds, such facts are thereby the measures we often apply to separate the "real" from the "unreal."

Resorting to "the facts of the case" is an important part of anyone's justification of his actions; resorting to hopes and preferences is just as important. But more important yet is the way we interweave both of these.

The illustration which I used in the above conversation (p. 70) is worth referring to again. For at least half

a century after Darwin, some supporters of the "free enterprise system" used the so-called facts of evolution to justify unregulated, dog-eat-dog competition. The weaknesses of such justification were exposed by other facts that were discerned by the promoters of antitrust laws in the late nineteenth century and by Keynesian, New Deal economists in the mid-twentieth century. But all along the facts of evolution could have been read differently than even Darwin read them—as Loren Eiseley shows us. Indeed, the intensity of the competitive impulse in nineteenth-century English economic theory and practice may even have shaped Darwin's own perception of the origin of species, and Loren Eiseley's attempt to correct popular interpretations of Darwin may owe something to the hopes that Eiseley brings to this subject as a late twentieth-century man.

There is probably no way to extricate our minds from the tangled network of both the "real" and the "ideal" in our attempts to evaluate this or that human action. This observation is not irrelevant theory; it is meant, in the midst of this study, to call our attention to a pair of questions critical to the process of ethical reflection. (1) How are the facts I see in this situation shaped by what I want to see? (2) How is what I want to see shaped by the facts? The first question will caution us against thinking that we can justify any human decision by reference to "unvarnished facts." The second will caution us against unvarnished ethical principles as well. *In ethical reasoning, facts and preferences need each other.*

4. The place of Christian faith in the ethical reflection of contemporary Christians is not always easy to discern.

Every person in the above dialogue is a member of some Christian church. We said in chapter 2 that if one wants to "begin with the beginning" of one's thinking about economic issues, he will have to begin with a religious faith. The dialogue suggests by its *silences* that on some occasions in the discussion of ethical issues contemporary Christians make few references to the alleged religious roots of their thinking. Even the theologians in this discussion infrequently use theological terms, references to the Bible, and the like. Should we conclude therefore that a religiously grounded ethic, a Hebrew-Christian faith in God as the beginning of ethical reflection, is impossible for our time? What about that confession of faith that ended chapter 1?

The answers to these questions are not easy. At least all the easy answers are suspicious. Apparently there is some deep-felt hesitancy on the part of many contemporary churchmen about readily prefacing their ethical reflections with phrases like, "God's will is . . ." or, "It says in the Bible that. . . ." At least twice in a portion of the same evening conversation some equivalent of the latter phrase is used, each time in a questioning mood wherein the speakers seem to ask: "How can we overcome or lessen the apparent antagonism and difference between the Biblical prophet's demand for justice and the way our modern economic system works?"

The reader is left to his own conclusions about this matter of how the roots of religious faith can be detected, if at all, in the above-ground ethical probings of Christians, but I will venture some provisional conclusions of my own.

On Believing in God in the Midst of Us

Joseph Addison paraphrased Psalm 19 in a famous eighteenth-century hymn to express a longtime Christian conviction about God:

". . . and everywhere that man can be,
Thou, God, art present there."

What is the relation of a faith like that to the process
of "ethical reflection" as Christians go about it? My own
personal answer would have to be: a deeply rooted faith
in Jesus Christ as the Lord of life releases the Christian
into the liberty of living in the power of the Spirit in all
the circumstances of life. Such faith may also rely on a
few solid outward helps (a Bible, a prayer, a sermon) as
necessary to guide human reflection on the great issues
of life. Faith is never so strong as to dispense with them.
But it is a sign of overconcentration upon the "means" of
grace and underconcentration upon the gracious Lord
himself if we do not, on some occasions, pitch into the
investigation of some human concern in the expectation
that God himself will be a present help, a sure spiritual
guide, in the midst of everything.

Much the same, by the way, needs to be said about
many other, less obviously "religious" helps to the living
of a human life: laws, rules, regulations, economic arrangements called systems. From the Christian perspective
none of these has the final word or final help for thinking
and doing "the right thing." The final word and final help
belong to God, "our refuge and strength" (Psalm 46:1).
His grace, his living Spirit is the final power that enables
us to make good judgments about anything in our life.
And the first liberating touch of God's Spirit frees a man
to plunge into the midst of life, to undertake the most
difficult of inquiries into the most "secular" of issues, because nothing human is merely secular anymore. Everything human is subject to the loving, powerful presence of
God.

If you believe that, you don't have to be responsible

for carrying God piggyback into every conversation. You are more likely to believe that, all along, "underneath are the everlasting arms," and you can forget about the *name* of God for a while because you know that God himself will not forget you! "You must work out your own salvation in fear and trembling; for it is God who works in you, inspiring both the will and the deed, for his chosen purpose" (Phil. 2:12-13, N.E.B.).

Questions for Further Reflection

1. Point out and discuss situations in your own life when, in your opinion, competition was a good thing, and other situations when competition was a bad thing.

2. Within the discussion, substantial emphasis was placed upon the value of competition between businesses. Do you think that competition between businesses *primarily benefits* the consumer by providing him with choices, or does competition *primarily harm* the consumer since each competitor is anxious to sell his product at the highest possible profit margin? Support your answer.

3. The conversationalists appear agreed that if technological advances or competition terminates or cripples the textile industry, then the government should relocate, retrain, and revitalize the people who have been affected. Do you think that the government has the same responsibility to relocate, retrain, and revitalize the nonskilled and semiskilled workers who are unemployed or underemployed as a result of changing labor needs? Why or why not?

4. Our speakers recognize the value of the government protecting the casualties of competition and helping to shape the business world toward greater justice for the poor. But what happens if the government and certain corporations arrange a mutually beneficial "partnership"—

such as many people think has come to exist in a "military-industrial-educational" complex? Who, then, protects the casualties and the poor? Or do you believe that such a "partnership" is unlikely? Why? Who is harmed when a contract for military equipment is cut back in an industry that employs thousands of people? Who might be benefited? How do you decide whom to permit to be benefited or harmed in such a "policy decision"?

5 | THE RICH AND THE POOR: What Is the Justice of God in an Unjust World?

In June of 1971 the General Assembly of the Presbyterian Church in the United States asked its member-constituents to study a paper, "American Christians and World Development." One section of this paper reads as follows:

. . . the economic gap between the rich and the poor is nothing unique to the modern world. The Bible and every other historical record attest to the existence of this gap in almost every civilization. The uniqueness of this gap in the twentieth century is twofold. First, modern technology, industrialism, and organization have vastly increased the prospect that a large proportion of the world's people might live well above the mere survival line. Heretofore in human history, the vast majority of people have been poor—that is, death from scarcity of material goods has been a threat that they have regularly reckoned with. Our Lord's prayer for "daily bread" must be understood in the context of a society whose members had long and anxiously sought protection from this threat. But modern industrialization has radically changed this situation for many a nearly-starving man on this planet. At least in his *mind* his situation has changed. It is now plain to growing numbers of very poor men that lifelong hunger, weakening diseases, and early death are not fates to which men *must* adjust. These are conditions that can be

changed; and of this the economically "developed"
countries of the world—Japan, Russia, Europe,
America—are dramatic proof. In these countries
basic economic wants are being met for the great
majority of the population to a degree without
precedent in the history of nations. The result is a
"revolution of rising expectations" among the poorer
people of the world. Once adjusted to their poverty
as an inevitability, they are no longer adjusted. . . .

. . . the rich nations of the world now live increasingly on fish-bowl display before the eyes of the
world's poor. The affluent societies are conspicuous
consumers, and the disparity between them and low-
consumption societies has become impossible to con-
ceal. Thus it is easy for poor people in the Southern
hemisphere to know that the rich nations of earth
are mostly in the Northern hemisphere. It is easy
for them to sense intuitively the truth in a comparison like this:

> If all the world were a community of 1000 peo-
> ple, 330 would be affluent and 670 would be
> poor, with tremendous variations in this affluence
> and poverty. Very generally, 63—mostly living
> in North America—would earn over $2,000 per
> year, with another 82—mostly living in Europe—
> earning between $1,000 and $2,000. But the vast
> majority of people (855) would earn less than
> $1,000 per year, and almost half (495) would
> earn less than $100 per year . . . 670 people
> would earn less than $300 per year.[6]

As part of that exceedingly privileged 63, we
Americans have limited knowledge and imagination
for understanding fully how the poor of the world

feel about the rich of the world. We are too rich to understand fully. We live in a country that produces annual goods and services—a Gross National Product —valued at one trillion dollars. In the 1960's, as a nation we *added* each year to that G.N.P. an amount equal to the *total* annual G.N.P. of all African countries put together. At present rates of consumption of food and other material goods in the two countries, the average American in his lifetime will consume at least 25 times as much as the average citizen of Indian.[7] It is a sad, puzzling fact about the way modern economic systems seem to work: the surpluses of the affluent everywhere multiply; the necessities of the poor are everywhere in short supply. It is easier for the typical American to buy a second car than for the typical Asian to feed his children.

As American Christians, few of us may be able to give an expert analysis of why the economic systems of the world are apparently in a state of growing, radical disparity. But we should be able to understand that, as islands of relative affluence in a worldwide sea of relative poverty, the rich nations of the world are targets of the cry: "Injustice!" Any Christian who has read the Old and the New Testament should be the first to hear that cry.

On Hearing the Cries of the Poor: Dialogue Continued

One of the interesting developments in the conversation excerpted in chapter 4 was the ease with which businessmen glided from the discussion of issues in the *American* economy into the discussion of issues in a *world* economy. This was not just a tribute to their breadth of mind. The businesses represented by these managers have trade relations with countries all over the world—Japan, Korea, Colombia, Yugoslavia, and India, to name five. Through trade relations with these countries the economy of my hometown, Raleigh, North Carolina, is intimately connected with a world economy. I cannot think concretely about the issues of my local or national economy, therefore, without thinking also about the web of economic exchange that binds my locale to those of millions of other people.

Nor can I think as a Christian about this tangled skein of economic relations without focusing upon a single outstanding feature of these relations: the gap between the enormously rich and the incredibly poor national economies.

A readiness to focus on the issue raised by this gap— What is the moral obligation of rich people living in the same society with poor people?—was shared by all of the persons quoted in chapter 4. They were anxious to face the issue in general terms—that is, on all levels of human society, from the situation of poor people living in our hometown to the situation of the poor in the developing nations.

A pivot point in that evening's discussion was reached when, in the examination of the assets and liabilities of a competitive economic system, the question was posed: *What are the obligations of an economic or political system to people who suffer loss from the impersonal operation of that system?* The first comment of a businessman in response to this question reminded the group of a conclusion reached in the first part of the discussion:

DELANEY: We have agreed, I think, that if through its economic aid programs the U.S. government strengthens the textile industry in, say, South America and Africa, then the government has the obligation to help the textile investor and the textile worker in this country to make the transition to other forms of productive enterprise.

SHRIVER: That suggests that we have a general moral question facing us about right relations between economically strong and economically weak people. The issue is: how can the weaker people in a world society become competitors with the stronger people, when the *means* for competing are already so disproportionately in the hands of the stronger?

DELANEY: One answer is that unless we foster the buying power of populations now poor, limits will be placed upon the capacity of the industrial system to grow. It is to the interest of the rich countries to develop consumer capability in the other countries.

SHRIVER: How about the development of competition capability, especially in areas where one has the world lead in sophisticated products? I understand that one U.S.-based corporation produces 80 percent of the world's computers. It may be all very well for African and Asian countries to make their own textile goods, but won't the West maintain its economic superiority by selling them machinery and electronic technology that they are unlikely to produce for a long time to come?

DELANEY: Not necessarily. We could all live to see the largest computer plant in the world located somewhere in Africa or Asia. The more freely economic decisions can be made on the basis of available resources of labor, land, raw materials, and the like, the more likelihood that sophisticated industry will move all over the world.

SHRIVER: And yet, for many of the sophisticated products of American industry, the markets have to be *other* sophisticated economies. We're beginning now, I understand, to sell computers to East Europeans and even Russians. In doing so, perhaps we give ourselves and them a key to yet larger wealth for Americans, Europeans, and Russians. But meantime, what good is the

computer industry to the African or South American
farmer? His economy is not touched by the enormous
new power of the computer. So the rich countries help
each other to get richer, and the poorer lag behind, not
really competing in the same economic "ball game." How
do the poor get on the bottom rung of the ladder that
leads to prosperity?

KELLER: Are you asking that in the world context?

SHRIVER: We could as easily ask it in our national context.
In our own city we have the beginnings of one of the
more sophisticated industrial-educational complexes in
the southeastern U.S. There's not too much of a future
around here for the unskilled person. A hundred years
ago the unskilled man had much better chances to avoid
poverty for the rest of his life. Today he has to have a
certain level of riches in hand—education, and capital
assets of other sorts as well—in order to *join* the "rich
society." Otherwise he is standing too far below the
ladder to reach its bottom rung.

Look, Lord,
I appreciate
what you've done
for me

but it's been a
profitable
relationship for
both of us—

a happy partnership!

DELANEY: In a truly competitive labor market, however, it will be to industry's advantage to remedy that situation. In my company, for example, five years ago we put on some intensive training programs to enable some local people to reach that bottom ladder rung. I remember some very sad days when I would have to sit down beside a job applicant and to help him print his name on the application.

KELLER: And today business runs an educational system that almost dwarfs the public education system. In our company we have a fifteen-week class going now for first-line supervisors on the rudiments of our economic system. In the past we have even taught reading and arithmetic. We do it to get the employees we must have to stay in business.

SHRIVER: Whenever there is a rise in unemployment or some technical substitute for untrained people, however, the least educated people suffer most. The man with least to sell is still the man most in danger of being bypassed by

You know I've done my part in making it. I've worked hard and been damned clever.

And now it's your turn. I expect you to keep things just as they are—but with less governmental interference

so I can enjoy what I've got.

the forces of the market. For example, unemployment
levels among *black* people in the U.S. are *twice* what
they are among whites. For a variety of reasons—from
poorly financed black schools to general prejudice in our
society—black people have had greater difficulty reaching
up to that bottom rung of the ladder. They *start off*
with fewer chances to get one of those jobs in your
factories, because you'll take the better qualified person
every time in preference to training an unqualified person.
Such people make the initially fatal mistake of being
born poor, as Michael Harrington said in the mid-sixties.
In the real world, the man who already has his million
or his social position is the one who from the beginning
is likely to be the strongest competitor.

EVERETT: Do we want to get everybody started out on just
the same plans? Do we want flat-out equality?

SHRIVER: We would have less trouble talking about "just
competition" if we *did* have something approaching
"equality of opportunity" in our society. Perhaps I'm
simply giving voice to a pervasive cry of injustice that
rises in the minds of the poor every time they are told
that America is "a land of opportunity." It improves
your economic opportunities in this country if you can
be born with a million dollars in your bank account!
Joseph Kennedy, you remember, presented each of his
children with a million dollars on their twenty-first birth-
days. That's quite a push toward getting elected senator
or president!

EVERETT: The trouble is that our whole system presupposes
that the people who are making money are the ones that
others want to encourage. Banks *want* to make loans
to companies that are making good profits, for that
means more secure loans, more assured profit for the
banks. Nobody would set out to start a bank precisely
for the purpose of making high risk loans, unless perhaps
the government or the church or some other agency
wants to do so. To be "in business" in our system is by
definition to be willing to stand the profit test.

SHRIVER: You would agree, then, that it is a fact of life that our system favors the strong and makes it hard for the weak.

EVERETT: Yes, it is a fact of life.

FOR REFLECTION

A real conflict is beginning to brew in this dialogue now: the "facts" of historic social-economic injustice *versus* the "facts" of the historic, biblically-rooted, Christian protest against that injustice. There is no question here about "lack of realism" on either side. It is two conflicting dimensions of reality that are at stake.

The prophets of the Old Testament saw the facts of economic injustice and claimed that these facts were under the judgment of God. And the practical issue for them, as for all men who believe in the justice of God, was what to do to rectify the injustice of men. The prophets would be interested, one suspects, in finding ways in which the poor man could borrow money at low interest rates. In modern American society, the poor borrow money at high interest rates—say, the 18 percent annual interest of most installment plans, a rate some business interests want to see doubled in my state. The poorer you are, the higher your interest rate in this system. Where is the justice in such a system? Perhaps it is just for the man who must take the greater risk of loaning money to the poor man, but the justice for the poor man himself is hard to see.

One of the problems of communication now plaguing the Protestant churches of America is connected to this whole discussion, by the way. Many people have some difficulty, for example, sitting in church and hearing ministers talk about economic and other injustices in contemporary society. Ministers spend several years in seminaries studying documents like the Old Testament. Then they come

out preaching sermons which make them sound like liberal
Democrats or socialists when they assert the justice in
government subsidies for the poor, low cost government
housing programs, and cooperative credit associations.
Such ministers seem not to appreciate the virtues of the
"competitive business system" as businessmen in their
congregation wish they did. They see those virtues as
hardly needing more defenders in a society which puts a
lot of power into the hands of business interests. "What
needs defending," they say, "are some other virtues like
compassion, pity for the weak, and justice for the poor.
If we can secure these virtues through the business system, then the controversy between the business ethic and
the Old Testament ethic might diminish. But it may be that
this is a standing controversy that cannot much be
diminished."

In the context of this study so far is a question de-
serving a lot of thought on the reader's part: what is the
role of the church in a society which, like all societies in
history, inflicts certain characteristic injustices upon the
poor? Is it useless for the church or Christians generally
simply to echo the cry "Unjust!"? Would it be better for
churchmen to work at (a) making the economic system
work better according to present rules, (b) changing and
improving the rules, (c) helping to invent a new system,
or (d) finding ways to take care of the casualties of the
system by charity, welfare, and the like? Is there any use
at all in the church's mere "speaking out" on these issues?

Whether the Biblical perspective is relevant at all to
the issues of a modern American economy, of course, is a
question that also must be wrestled with. As you think
about this question, you might reflect on various forms of
relevance, such as the relevance of the *ultimately right*

as well as the relevance of the *currently possible*. In the Bible, prophets are sometimes only "voices crying in the wilderness." But was that not better than no voice at all crying out for the needs of the poor?

PART II

DELANEY: You know, it's almost strange to be using the Old Testament as a guideline in the matters before us now. Economic systems now are radically different. I don't know how to fit the Bible into all of this.

KELLER: Even assuming the relevance of the Bible on some points, the thing that worries me is whether you can test everything about an economic system by what it does to the low man on the totem pole. Red Blount used to say that everybody talks about 4 percent unemployed and nobody talks about 96 percent employed. Furthermore, when you center your concern on the very poorest people, you may neglect the people several notches up. If earnings on stocks decline, or if inflation grows, for example, the pensions of a lot of retired school teachers and widows will be affected. The system may not benefit everybody equally, but it benefits a lot more people than used to be benefited. For myself, I have some confidence that this economic system is *evolving* towards justice for more people than have ever had a slice of affluence. To make that more certain, our society has imposed some of these rules or restraints already mentioned.

McCRARY: The case for that may be a little easier to make within the U.S. than in the international context. If Ivan Illich is right, our whole country's economy benefits from selling our sophisticated industrial products abroad —and the lowest paid worker in *our* factories benefits from this. But do the mass of poor men in other countries get much benefit? The very thrust of our system requires us to reach out for markets for what we happen to be producing; so, in Illich's phrase, you have tractors built in America to serve the tastes of affluent American farmers. You have our salesmen selling such tractors to the South Americans, who need a life-long tractor that is not yet being produced *any*where. Can our system come to terms with the basic needs of populations whose values may be different from our own?

DELANEY: The most impressive thing about that Illich article to me was the thought that somebody should give his attention to the production of that lifelong tractor—that mechanical mule. If it's such a real need of peasants in South America, why don't we invent one, and produce it or help them to produce it?

SHRIVER: Suppose we produced a truly lifelong tractor that wouldn't wear out for fifty years. Wouldn't that mean that you would run out of a market for tractors rather quick?

KELLER: Not if you could convince the farmer that you had some better ideas for a new tractor. Selling the farmer on your better tractors is part of industrial expansion.

SHRIVER: So that if you want to criticize Ivan Illich, you will have to say that it is no crime to try to persuade another man to buy your products, and that the other man should be the judge of his own need. Illich is saying that the other man in Latin America does not need a Coke as much as he needs pure water, that he doesn't need fancy hospitals as much as public health clinics in villages, that he doesn't need your obsolescence-prone tractor as much as he needs a mechanical mule. But some peasant in South America just might give Illich the put-down by saying: "Let *me* be the judge of all that."

KELLER: Yes, and the leaders of these nations often say the same. A few years ago, every developing country had to have its steel mill as a sign of its "arrival" in the modern age. Or an airline, or a big dam. ·If the leaders say that is what they want, who are we in this country to say "no"?

SHRIVER: Maybe this is just another context in which to raise the same question that has haunted this whole discussion: *for whose sake does industrial growth take place?* Electricity consumption in this country has been rising about 100 percent every decade. So far as I know similar rates of growth hold in Russia, Europe, and Japan. We in America now use about half of the world's electricity. All of Asia, with half the world's population, uses some 10 percent of the world's electricity. Two billion of the world's 3.5 billion people consume no electricity at all! Here we are in the richer parts of the world increasing our use of electricity by leaps and bounds, polluting our environment in the process, while the consumption rate of the world's poor is still very low.

DELANEY: That's a very interesting admission on your part. Electricity is certainly one of the bases for building an industrialized society. Spurred on by the dynamics of growth and competition, this society has produced more and more electricity, and for doing so has sought more and more sources of fuel. Competition for fuel sources has finally led us to a source that is everywhere abundant—the power of the atom. The transition from water to fossil to atomic power has now made it possible for the developing nations, if they wish, to leap immediately into nuclear generation of electricity. And nuclear power will probably be kinder to the natural environment than coal-powered generators ever were.

SHRIVER: Did we *know* that there would be such a new source of energy when we began to exploit the world's supplies of oil and gas for our own fuel needs in America and Europe?

DELANEY: No, we didn't. But we did discover something in a competitive economic framework that will prove enormously useful to the countries coming later upon the economic scene.

SHRIVER: Well, even if one ignores the fact that this development of atomic power was greatly accelerated by political conflicts in World War II, your version of the blessings of our industrial system looks like super-optimism to me. Roughly translated, your view seems to say: "Let's push this selective development and growth of our national economy, because eventually it's going to work out for the benefit of the people who right now are left behind. We don't know how, but we have a mystical assurance that it is so." The Bible might paraphrase such a view as: "Let us continue sinning that grace may abound!" That's putting it too strongly. But I can't avoid the thought that there is some sin involved in living in the country that owns 50 percent of the world's wealth while having 6 percent of the world's people.

DELANEY: I don't consider that sinning, I'm afraid.

SHRIVER: It looks, on the face of it, like a standing *inequity*.

DELANEY: I guess it comes down to asking if any country should hold up its own growth while waiting or working to get the other up to its own level. That might just prove to be economically impossible.

SHRIVER: Okay, look at the international economic system from this oversimplified perspective for a minute: in Liberia, the foundation of the economy is a huge rubber plantation system owned mostly by American companies. The daily wage of rubber workers in that country is less than a dollar. Now here we are in the United States using rubber products made from Liberian raw materials. What defense do we have against the widespread accusation that we are supporters of a system that exploits the Liberian rubber workers?

DELANEY: I think the best defense is that economics is only *one side* of a society; you can't expect the economic system to cure the total problems of society. Some of these problems will be reflected in economic terms, but some of the economic problems can only be solved through adjustments outside the economic environment.

The political and social systems are partly responsible for how the economic forces work. Doesn't the Liberian government have responsibility for securing loans from the World Bank for industrial diversification or for negotiating trade arrangements that may build a healthier economy in that country? And if the leaders of the country profit from the present arrangement, while the poor are only modestly benefited, why should American consumers shoulder the blame for the inequity? Perhaps we could pay a few more dollars for our rubber products, but there is no economic mechanism for us to do so for the sake of those *workers*. The market system in raw materials by itself will not be the major source of more equity for those workers.

SHRIVER: Now that does make sense to me. The remedy for economic injustice, then, is not merely in the economic system; it may lie as much in political and social structures. Only I would add: it may also lie in the realm of our ideas of what kind of a society we *want* with our fellowmen. All these rules we've talked about that put certain restraints upon the free working of systems, and the new institutions like the World Bank and the Peace Corps are social *inventions* that had their partial beginning in the spirit of people who say: "This is the kind of improvement that *ought* to be striven for in human affairs." That's beginning with a vision of the criteria by which the presently real world should be judged and with a hope that the vision might become reality through sufficiently dedicated human effort. Such vision and such hope are the foundation of ethics. What a man sees as desirable in human affairs and what he hopes for enough to give his own effort to achieving— *that* is his real ethic.

KELLER: I would agree with that, but I'm not sure we are doing justice yet to *the relation of self-interest to other people's interests,* say, in the structure of American economic aid policies. For example, most of our aid programs have in them a "Buy American" provision. As a taxpayer, I believe that this is perfectly just. Why should I be asked to subsidize competition for American business in other countries? That they should be allowed to *compete* with American business is another matter. The A.I.D. money is my tax money, so I have every right to say that it should be spent in my interest.

SHRIVER: That view rather dismays me. You have every obligation from a Christian standpoint to be sure that it is also spent in the interest of other people!

KELLER: No, the *other* side of my view is that our government should also appropriate funds for the World Bank, which in turn can subsidize industries around the world. This is one of John Delaney's adjustments *outside* the competitive system. When through artificial subsidy these industries grow strong, then they enter the competitive world market along with everybody else.

SHRIVER: But that is a strange retreat from your previous viewpoint. It's still American tax dollars going into the World Bank.

KELLER: The difference is that in the World Bank the nations of the world are spreading the risk around. And the World Bank can make more responsible judgments about needs around the world than can the U.S. alone. What we *can* judge in any aid *we* give directly is our own self-interest. The A.I.D. program is and should be a device for moving American products into the world market. I will concede that we must make it possible for industry in the poorer countries at least to get into the world market. We must make it possible for them to play the game, so to speak, to pursue their self-interest in competitive terms. The competitive game I would leave to the "fight of the gladiators," but now with the gladiators equally armed.

SHRIVER: A very arresting way of putting your two-sided view! What you say sets off a train of reflection in me as a churchman. I think it is a *long* train of reflection, so could I presume your patience a bit? In this study book that you are helping me write, suppose that as joint authors we should say that economic competition may indeed work to the advantage of many parties, but not of all parties. And suppose we reiterate my contention that the protection of *injured parties* is a profound, unfailing emphasis of the Christian ethic. What we seem to be suggesting, then, is a combination of hard competition between the strong along with a program for being sure that the weak really can compete.

Then the question that concerns me the most is: what kind of an economic or other "world development" program should the *Christians* of this country help *invent?* Can we invent a system that reduces the number of injured parties, so that we can, in effect, move from an "ambulance ethic" to an "accident prevention ethic"?

To be specific: my government spends my tax dollars on some purposes that I regard as waste—our ten-year-old war in Southeast Asia, for example. When will the government and other large organizations I belong to (like the church) come up with a program that demands money from me for some worthier purposes? Right now my government spends about 2 billion dollars a year on "foreign aid." That's less than a *penny* out of every Federal income tax dollar coming out of my paycheck! Granted that on the personal level I do not want to reduce my income by the enormous slice that might be necessary if the U.S. became a socialist state. But granted too that there are some hundreds of dollars in my personal budget that I could feel *morally obligated* to devote to the development of the economics of poorer nations around the world, the same obligation I could feel for a more adequate welfare program for poor people who live inside this country. We don't much have such programs, such a policy, such an aim in this country.

True, if you told me in order to help the world's

poor I would have to reduce my personal income by 75 percent, I would (like every other self-interested, middle-class American) probably recoil. I would find that I am just too much a sinner and not enough a saint for such a move. But suppose you came to me and said, "It is going to cost you as much as 10 percent of your annual income, Christian friend, to put your money where your mouth is." I would listen hard to that. It would not be a *very* sacrificial demand, would it? It would mean a slight reform in my spending habits, much too slight to be anything close to "revolutionary." Much closer to revolution was Jesus' demand of the rich young ruler that he give it all up and become a disciple.

There are many in the world, of course, who would laugh at such a reform proposal, because, they say, "the whole capitalist system works consistently to the disadvantage of the poor in the world. Give your 10 percent or give half of your earnings from the world market, and you will still be a part of an exploiting system!" That analysis is not one which I can altogether

Don't talk to me about rights, boy.   Don't pester taxpayers for handouts.

ignore or altogether accept. But I can accept the neces-
sity for Americans, especially Christian Americans, to
make more than token gestures toward "arming the
gladiators in the world equally." We have a terribly long
way to go before that happens.

EVERETT: We might even be persuaded to such sacrifices on
the basis of long-range self-interest. After all, it is to
our interest to live in a world where people are not always
at each other's throats.

SHRIVER: What an unbeatable combination for effecting
change in a human society! To do a thing because it is
not only right but also beneficial to oneself!

DELANEY: In this connection, I think we are undergoing some
fantastic changes in the perception of our self-interest
through a worldwide communication system. Some
Pakistani, for example, were reported to be amazed at
the worldwide attention given their 1970 cyclone disaster.
"Why," they said, "we've been suffering from these things
for centuries. Why all the excitement all of a sudden?"

You're right, I think, to suggest that there is some

It's all we can do to pay for this city's riot protection.

untapped willingness to respond to world need among
many people, if they can be shown the need and a well-
conceived program to meet the need. In fact, that's one
of the troubles with the principle, "Love thy neighbor
as thyself." So many of my neighbors I have no ac-
quaintance with. I can sympathize with my neighbor the
textile worker in Henderson, N.C., much more easily
than with my neighbor the textile worker in Africa.
Then occasionally a cyclone comes along, and I get
some images of my neighbor in Pakistan.

MCCRARY: Which suggests the possibility that with increasing
communication in the world it will be increasingly possible for one person to identify his "self-interest" with
the interest of many other selves. We begin to *define*
ourselves in relation to other selves. We see ourselves as
entangled with each other.

DELANEY: Yes, why are we reluctant to admit that having
a clear conscience at night, knowing that the world might
be a little better because of what we did that day, is
not in our self-interest?

FOR REFLECTION

The Justice of God and the Justice of Men

The Delaneys, Everetts, Kellers, McCraries, and
Shrivers of this world have no easy time securing for themselves a clear conscience—in either of two senses. On the
one hand, they cannot be sure that they clearly *know*
what are the right, good, and proper things to do about
the problems of poor people in a lopsidedly rich world.
On the other hand, they cannot be sure that they have
clearly *done* what they already know to do. Indeed, some
of our ethical talk above could be called a substitute for
ethical action. How easy it is to imagine some poor man
from a slum breaking into our middle-class living room

and crying out: "Stop all this polite conversation and face up to our misery! Give us food, not talk! Give us your Christian action, not your Christian ethics! Give us justice, not your chatter about economic systems!"

Such impatience with mere talk is well taken. The Bible portrays a similar impatience in Amos, who heaped scorn upon pious religious talk used by the rich as a cloak over their exploitation of the poor (Amos 2:6-8, 5:21-24). There was a like impatience in Jesus, who condemned outright the people who made hollow pretensions of loyalty to him ("Lord, Lord!") and did not do what he commanded (Luke 6:46). All through the Bible, justice is a *deed;* it is not a mere concept. And all through the Bible, the time for talk about justice is usually short. Instructions for right living, in economic and other human affairs, often comes across in simple, straightforward terms:

> He has showed you, O man, what is good; and what does the LORD require of you but to do justice, and to love kindness, and to walk humbly with your God? (Micah 6:8)

> Sell all that you have and distribute to the poor, and you will have treasure in heaven; and come, follow me. (Luke 18:22)

> If you really fulfil the royal law, according to the scripture, "You shall love your neighbor as yourself," you do well. (James 2:8)

Without question, the more serious a Bible reader you happen to be, and the more serious a Christian, the clearer should be certain things about economic justice for the poor in the modern world. We should not have to argue over simplicities like:

God will judge the whole world of men according to
what compassion men had upon their most needy
neighbors. (See Matt. 25:31-46.)

It is wrong for some to feast while others starve. (See
Luke 16:19.)

More can be done to bring some measure of justice
in the world than is presently being done; we have
not done all we can do; I have not done all I can
do. (Choose your own text!)

One of the effects of these "simplicities" is that they
drive a sensitive person to his knees:

We have left undone those things which we ought to
have done; And we have done those things which
we ought not to have done; And there is no health
in us.[8]

In fact, simple guidelines for behavior can be occasions
for much inward misery for the sensitive religious man. We
don't obey even the simplest instructions. So how is sim-
plicity alone of sufficient help to us?

But as a matter of Christian faith, the whole subject of our checkered human justice in relation to divine
justice is covered over by some *merciful complexities*—
or so the Bible claims. It is risky to take refuge in complexity, but not to do so may be even riskier.

Take the complexity of the very notion of *God's
justice*. A judge of a court in my hometown says, "I am
always afraid of giving people the impression that I know
what justice is. In a courtroom, the best that we can do is
to *seek* justice. Perfect justice always seems to elude us."
This is also true in the Bible; human justice at best is
a pretty rough copy of the real thing—God's justice. In

fact, the foundation of the Christian's search for a just social order is his confidence that what is currently impossible with men is ultimately possible with God. Marx was wrong in believing that the religious man's hope for a better world, wherein God's justice is triumphant, is always a substitute for an attempt to make the world better now. Sometimes it is only the Christian's faith that God can bring ultimate healing to the world's pain, beyond human ability to do so, that keeps the Christian trying to do what he can do.

A second merciful complexity, akin to the first, is the Christian's confidence in God as *the Lord of human history*. As we look out upon the world of economic relations between the nations, we are called to think theologically as well as ethically; that is, we are called not only to consider what we should do but also to perceive what God may be doing, quite without our help, to "put down the mighty from their thrones," to exalt "those of low degree," to fill "the hungry with good things," and to send the rich "empty away" (Luke 1:52-53). That the poor of the world are undergoing their own revolution of rising expectations, for example, may be one of the unintended results of the industrial revolution in the West. Must we not credit to the strange power of God the impatience of the world's poor with all the systems that falsely pretend to be their saviors—communism, capitalism, nationalism? Is not the Lord of history behind the "grassroots" protest of the poor man against the feasting of his rich neighbors?

Then, finally, there is the merciful complexity of *the forgiveness of God*. It is not much the fashion nowadays to believe in a God who either judges or forgives human sin. But for the Christian, there are two terrible things that would make the world unlivable: if there were no

judgment of God (then the wrongs of the world would
have no sure condemnation) or if there were only judgment in God (then the wrongs in us all would result in the
condemnation of us all).

The faith that keeps us thinking, conversing, acting,
and repenting about the tangled world of relationships between the rich and the poor is this:

> —*That God does judge men and societies for their
> injustice to the poor* (the poor have hope, there-
> fore; the Judge of all the earth is on *their* side).
> —*That God does forgive men and societies for their
> injustices* (we all have hope, too, for the Judge
> is also on *our* side).

A great mystery . . . how God can be the "loyal
opposition" of rich men. By world standards, almost every
person reading this page is a rich man, so more than most
men living we have reason to hope that God forgives the
sins of the rich, too.

Questions for Further Reflection

1. Everett, Shriver, Delaney, and McCrary con-
cluded this discussion by suggesting that perhaps self-
interest could be combined with our sense of justice for
the poor, and everyone would profit. Do you think that
the "competitive spirit" would tolerate this "soft" approach? Why do you think Keller dropped out of the discussion at this point?

2. If we firmly believe that we as affluent individuals
and as an affluent nation have a moral obligation to share
our wealth and resources with the less fortunate, how do
we best encourage our corporations, our churches, and our
government to act according to this moral judgment?

6 POSTSCRIPT: The Pilgrimage of Christian Ethical Reflection

There is an apathy born of comfort, but there is also an apathy born of complexity. One can be overwhelmed by problems as well as taken over by vested interests. Threatened by the demands of freedom and by the awesomeness of our decisions, we are prone to echo Estragon's reply in Beckett's *Waiting for Godot*.
Vladimir: "Well? What do we do?"
Estragon: "Don't let's do anything; it's safer." [9]

The diligent reader of this book would be justified, I think, in putting it down with a profound sense of confusion. Perhaps you picked it up in the expectation that you would be told here what ethical judgments to make upon current issues in American economic life. Instead you have been told:

—that authoritative judgments on economic issues are few and far between;
—that Christians disagree quite a bit on such matters;
—that there are some major guidelines for Christian ethical judgments from the Bible, but no one is solely sufficient for the making up of one's mind on economic issues;
—that Christians must seek to give justice and compassion a shape in the world of complex economic systems;
—that the *search* for justice and compassion may be

as important as any of their present institutional *expressions;*

—that ultimate justice and compassion belong to God, not men;

—that ultimate guidance in these matters is in the Holy Spirit, not in the minds of men.

To be told this may be to get both less and more than you expected: less, because it might be nice to have "the answers"; more, because to have the range of suggestions above is to make the whole business of moving toward answers full of so many considerations.

A word about answers, and another about multiple considerations, before we end this particular conversation.

The Answer: You

Scholars who have studied the history of ethics very carefully call attention to a remarkable feature of the

ethic that goes by the name "Christian." Many ethical systems among the famous cultures of men—the Greeks, the Romans, the Chinese, the Hindus—are exceedingly attentive to our need for ethical *wisdom*. The aim of some of these systems is to provide their disciples with authoritative *knowledge* of proper human behavior. One distinctive feature of ethics in the New Testament, and in many other ethical writings of Christians down through history, is a focus on the need of man for a transformation of his *personal capacity*. The New Testament abounds in the claim that unless men acquire a "new heart," unless they "repent," unless they become "new creatures," no amount of mere wisdom will make them into proper human beings who "love their neighbors as themselves."

Much of the dialogue quoted in this book apparently shies away from a very basic claim about Christian ethics: what counts is not just being *wise* enough to understand complicated ethical problems, but being *personally transformed* enough to want to act ethically with all one's heart, strength, and mind. We came close to this insight when one of us confessed that he is not "saint" enough to give up much more than 10 percent of his income for the world's poor (p. 98). It may be fairly clear—in principle —that an incredibly rich country like the United States should do a lot more for the world's poor than it is doing. What is not so clear is the ability of even the Christian people of this nation to *want* to do what they sense they *should* do, according to the ethical principles of their own religious tradition.

The intellectual problem is not thereby eliminated, but in Christian ethics it is demoted to secondary consideration. The question of what kind of a foreign aid or welfare program would actually serve the needs of the poor is indeed an important intellectual problem. It calls for a far better mobilization of the intelligence of government, science, business, and the churches than is yet being mustered. But, again, from the Christian perspective, *the* ethical problem is not man's ignorance. The problem is man himself.

This may help us to understand somewhat the strange *variety* of Jesus' treatment of "economic questions" in his teachings and in his dealings with people, as reported in the Gospels. His readiness to pay attention to the physical needs of people was an early reason why his "fame spread everywhere" (Mark 1:28). Far from minimizing economic questions, his parables are full of incidents involving money, buying and selling, saving and wasting, eating and building. (Note for example Matt. 13:45-46; Luke 12:18; 15:8, 12.) But, while he said to a rich man, "sell all that you have" (Luke 18:22), he commended (by implication) some men who conserved money (Matt. 25:28), and to his disciples on one occasion (Matt. 26:12) he said that there are better uses of expensive perfume than selling it for the sake of the poor! How do we account for this almost casual variety of specific instructions to people concerning their relation to material goods? One answer is surely this: precisely because "a man's life does not consist in the abundance of his possessions" (Luke 12:15), Jesus was free to concentrate his teachings and his ministry upon the basic questions of men's *whole-hearted love of God and their neighbors.* His specific instructions to the rich young man (an example that gave us much discomfort in chapter 3) apparently were aimed at loosening that man's devotion to wealth and transferring it to God and his neighbor. It was a question of where that man's basic, heartfelt *treasure* was to be "located." "For where your treasure is, there will your heart be also" (Matt. 6:21).

So some say that Jesus did not have an *economic* ethic; what he offered men was a deep, pervasive, transforming of their deepest loyalties. After that transformation, the most important question of economics, politics, family, and every other "sector" of human life was *settled*.

In this context it makes sense for the Christian to believe that, in his attempt to make a judgment upon economic issues in his nation's life, the issue-within-all-issues is: "To whom am I chiefly loyal? Where is my true treasure, that determines where my heart is?" To the extent that the answer is "God and my neighbor" a Christian can claim to be ready to *think* about the *other* issues in ethical judgment-making. Then also it will be clear to him that "the answer" to ethical questions is more a certain kind of man than a certain kind of wisdom.

That, by the way, is only a reaffirmation of the basis for the freedom-to-inquire that has been assumed throughout these pages. Once he has gotten the question of some basic loyalties straight, the Christian finds that he has been liberated to do some exploring of his own life and the life of his time. "Work out your own salvation . . ." (Phil. 2:12-13) is the instruction given men who have been "oriented" to the night by their recognition of the North Star and to the day by the slant of the noonday sun. They know "which way is up," and they can be generally trusted to find their way where known paths are few without getting lost.

Living in Many Dimensions

The liberty to explore the new, historically unprecedented issues facing modern man in his economic affairs is also the liberty to "take on" the multiple factors inherent in those affairs. We have met this multiplicity repeatedly, often enough to discourage even the stouthearted, to bring

us to the verge of "apathy born of complexity." Who are
we to understand, much less to improve, foreign aid programs? tariff policies? the plight of the unmechanized
farmer in Peru? the plight of the poor man in a ghetto in
our own hometown? The answer is: we *are* the ones to
try to understand and to try to be neighbors to a world of
people, *if* we are the people whose loyalty has been fixed,
once and for all, upon the God and Father of our Lord
Jesus Christ. Not to try to love all our neighbors would
be to contradict the chief fact of our lives: "We love, because he first loved us" (1 John 4:19).

The strength to live a many-dimensioned life is here.
Something about our time calls for us to acquire that
strength, does it not? In a 1970 best seller, *Future Shock,*
Alvin Toffler portrays the danger that in a complex,
rapidly changing society many people will find it impossible to cope with change. They may find it necessary
to retreat from complexity, to crawl into some sort of
psychological hole.

Surely there are limits on any person's ability to
keep himself oriented in the midst of confusion, but it is
proper to suppose that the people who really know which
is the Pole Star will not be disoriented by a bright and
starry night. People have to know which way is North,
which way is "right," which way is "good," in order to
move from any familiar place to any unfamiliar place;
this is true whether you are an astronaut on your way to
Mars or an American citizen on your way to being part
of civilization's first really global economic system.

Indeed, the basic orientation of the Christian—his
conviction that God loves him and that he is to love his
neighbor—is his foundation for coping with far more
than mere complexity. Sin, death, and every possible evil
can now be coped with; if none of these enemies of our

composure can "separate us from the love of God" (Rom. 8:39), how shall the tangled confusions of "issues in the American economy" do so?

The important ethical point of it all is that, secure in this faith, a man is also secure to undertake his own adventurous explorations of such issues, no matter how complex they may be. It has been the purpose of this study to make you bolder for undertaking your own adventures of reflection, decision, and action in relation to the economic issues in your life as an American. In the hope that some success has attended the purpose, on behalf of all your fellow explorers who have contributed to the study I wish you . . . good adventuring!

NOTES

1. Dorothy Lee, *Freedom and Culture* (Englewood Cliffs, N.J.: Prentice-Hall, 1959), p. 163.
2. Waldo Beach, *The Christian Life* (Richmond: The CLC Press, 1966), p. 12.
3. The names of people other than the writer quoted in these and other dialogues in this book are fictitious, but descriptions of the people are accurate, as are quotations ascribed to them. In some instances the transcript has been edited for conciseness, but most of it is verbatim.
4. Ivan Illich, "Outwitting the 'Developed' Countries," *The New York Review of Books,* 1969.
5. Loren Eiseley, *The Unexpected Universe* (New York: Harcourt Brace & World, Inc., 1969), pp. 184-185.
6. Richard Dickinson, *Line and Plummet: The Churches and Development* (Geneva: The World Council of Churches, 1968), p. 11.
7. Wayne H. Davis, "Overpopulated America," *The New Republic,* January 10, 1970, pp. 13-15.
8. *The Book of Common Worship* (Philadelphia: Board of Christian Education of the Presbyterian Church in the U.S.A., 1946), p. 21.
9. C. Eric Mount, Jr., "The Squint," *Sometimes They Cry,* ed. Estelle Rountree and Hugh F. Halverstadt (New York: Friendship Press, Inc., 1970), p. 110.